FILING and COMPUTER DATABASE PROJECTS

Jeffrey R. Stewart, Ed.D.
Educational Consultant

GLENCOE
McGraw-Hill
New York, New York   Columbus, Ohio   Woodland Hills, California   Peoria, Illinois

Filing and Computer Database Projects

Imprint 1999

Send all inquiries to:

Glencoe/McGraw-Hill
936 Eastwind Drive
Westerville, Ohio 43081

ISBN 0-02-801029-9

Printed in the United States of America.

4 5 6 7 8 9 0 073 03 02 01 00 99

CONTENTS

PROJECT SIX: BURGER BARN

FANFILE

FILING AND COMPUTER DATABASE PROJECTS

INTRODUCTION

The six projects in this practice set give you an opportunity to work with both manual files and computer databases.

Projects 1 and 2 deal with card filing and correspondence filing. In these projects, you will practice indexing, alphabetizing, filing, decision making, and correspondence management.

Projects 3 through 6 involve a use of the data disk and an electronic database to manage records electronically. In these projects, you will work with a customer file, a client file, an inventory file, and an employee file.

FILING PROJECTS

In Projects 1 and 2 of this practice set, you will work to develop the following competencies:

1. Using a simulated card file, you will file records alphabetically according to the rules for alphabetic filing. These rules, with application practice, appear in Chapter 5 of the textbook *Professional Records Management*. The rules also appear in this workbook beginning on page 19.
2. Using a simulated card file, you will file records by number, by geographic location, and by subject.
3. Using items of correspondence, you will make decisions as to which items to file and what further action to take. You will organize these records alphabetically and by subject. You will also practice cross-referencing selected items of correspondence.

Each of the 12 numbered assignments in the filing projects is designed to be completed in approximately one hour. Project 1 (Assignments 1–8) includes alphabetic, numeric, geographic, and subject card filing. Project 2 (Assignments 9–12) includes alphabetic and subject correspondence filing.

PROJECT ONE

CARD FILING

ASSIGNMENT 1 ALPHABETIC FILING OF INDIVIDUAL NAMES, CARDS 1–32

You are a new employee in the sales office of Jacobsen's Department Store in Spanish Lake, Missouri. Jacobsen's is a successful, locally owned business with one large store. Your responsibilities include filing customer names alphabetically according to Filing Rules 1 through 5.

For this assignment, you will use cards that have the numbers 1 through 32 in the upper-right corner. These numbers are for *identification only*; they are not part of the records. You will also use **FanFile,** which is a cardboard sheet that is folded to form a desk file to make it easier to do your work.

Read each step carefully, and complete the step before you continue.

1. *Set up FanFile*. Remove *FanFile* from this workbook, and fold along the scores so it looks like Illustration 1.

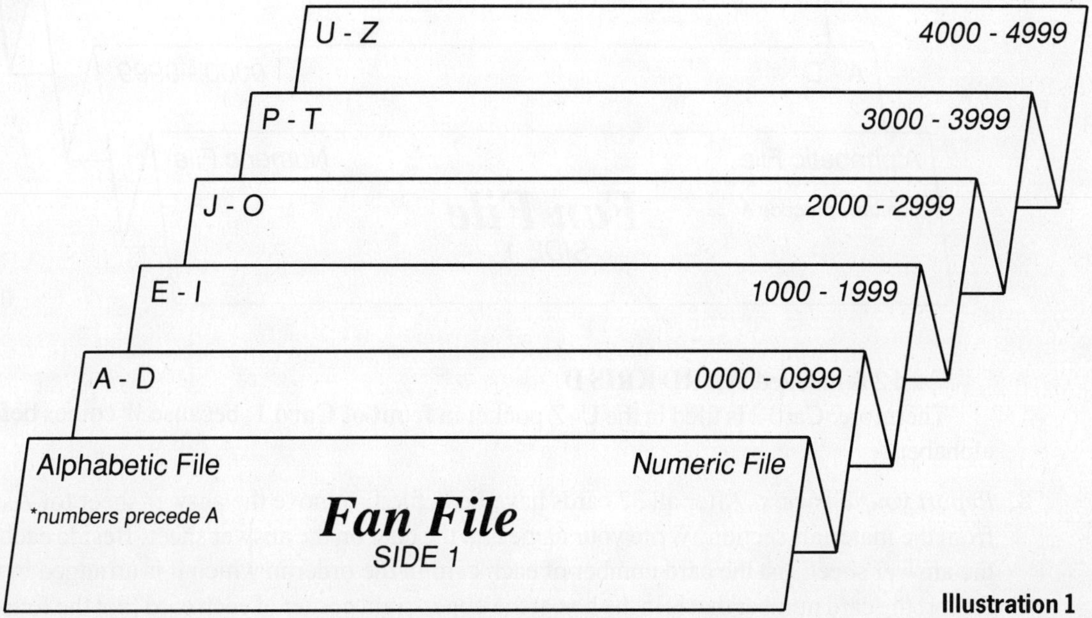

Illustration 1

Place *FanFile* in front of you so that Side 1 is facing you as shown in the illustration. Note that there are five pockets in *FanFile*. Each pocket has a caption at the left for alphabetic filing: A–D, E–I,

J–O, P–T, and U–Z. The caption *A–D* means that names having first units beginning with *A, B, C,* or *D* are filed under that caption. The other four captions have the same meaning for their range of letters. For this assignment, you will file the cards in alphabetic order in the five pockets.

2. *Detach sheets with cards 1–32*. Remove the two sheets from the materials section of this workbook. These sheets have cards with the numbers 1 through 32 in the upper-right corners. Do not separate the individual cards yet.
3. *Review*. If you are familiar with Filing Rules 1 through 5, proceed to the next step. If not, review Rules 1 through 5 in your textbook (Chapter 5) or on page 19 of this workbook.
4. *Organize your materials*. Place the two sheets that you removed from this workbook in front of you. Card numbers 1 through 16 on the first sheet and cards 17 through 32 on the second sheet should be facing up. Ignore the cards on the backs of the two sheets. They will be used in Assignment 2.
5. *Index*. Index each of the 32 names by writing or keying the names in indexed order on the line above each name. The first card has been indexed for you as an example. Remember to use all capital letters and to omit any punctuation.
6. *Separate* the 32 cards at the perforations. Arrange them in order from 1 through 32.
7. *File alphabetically*. File each card in correct alphabetic order in the appropriate pocket of *FanFile*. File each card to the right of its caption so the caption remains visible. For example:

   Card 1 is indexed **ZOLLER LINDA J**

   Therefore: Card 1 is filed in the U–Z pocket to the right of the U–Z caption as shown in Illustration 2.

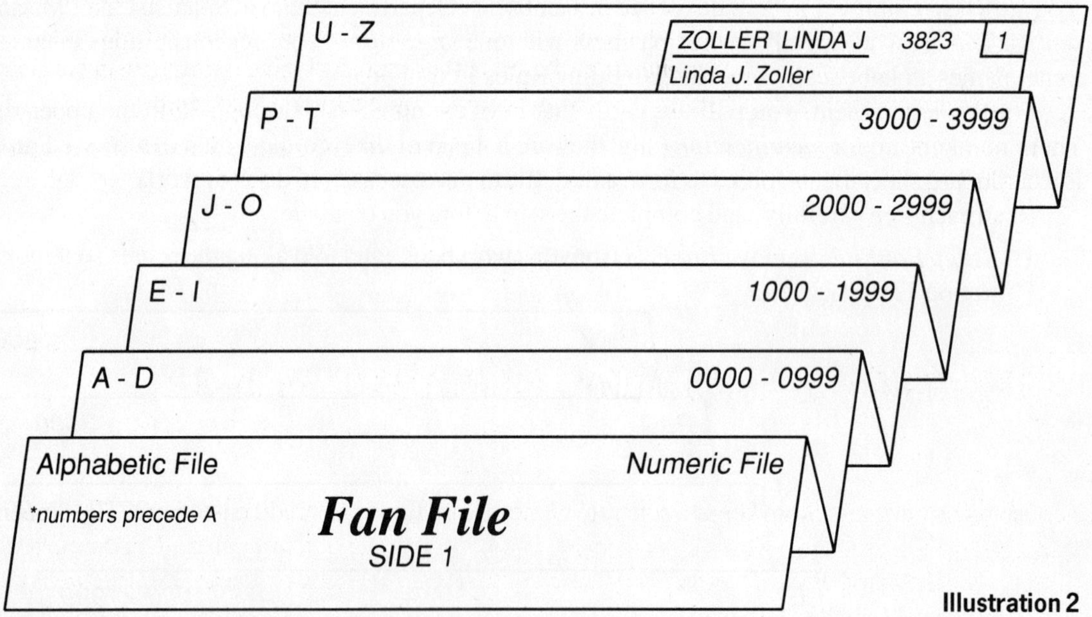

Illustration 2

   Card 2 is indexed **WARD KRIS D**

   Therefore: Card 2 is filed in the U–Z pocket **in front of Card 1**, because *W* comes before *Z* in the alphabet.

8. *Report your answers*. After all 32 cards have been filed, remove the answer sheet for Assignment 1 from the materials section. Write your name and the date on the answer sheet. Beside each caption on the answer sheet, list the card number of each card in the order in which it is arranged in the pocket. Report the card number that is in the box at the upper-right corner of each card (not the four-digit number that also appears on each card). As an example, all of the numbers for the A–D caption are listed on the answer sheet for you. Be sure that your answers are the same as the example.

9. *Conclude Assignment 1*. Hand in the answer sheet to your instructor. Remove the 32 cards from the five pockets of *FanFile*. Store them in one of the disk pockets in the back of this workbook. They will be used again in Assignment 2.

ASSIGNMENT 2 ADDITIONAL ALPHABETIC FILING OF INDIVIDUAL NAMES, CARDS 33–64

1. *Assemble your materials.* Retrieve the 32 cards used in Assignment 1 from the pocket in the back of this workbook. Numbers 33 through 64 appear on the back (shaded side) of these 32 cards. Arrange these cards in order from 33 through 64.
2. *Set up FanFile*. Place *FanFile* in front of you so Side 1 is facing you.
3. *Index*. Index each of the 32 names by writing or keying the names in indexed order on the line above each name.
4. *File alphabetically*. File each card in alphabetic order in the appropriate pocket of *FanFile*. File each card to the right of its caption.
5. *Report your answers*. After all 32 cards have been filed, remove the answer sheet for Assignment 2 from the materials section. Write your name and date on the answer sheet. Beside each caption on the answer sheet, list the card number of each card in the order in which it is arranged in the pocket. Report the card number that appears in the box in the upper-right corner of each card.
6. *Conclude Assignment 2.* Hand in the answer sheet to your instructor. Remove the 32 cards from the pockets of *FanFile.* Store them in the pocket in the back of this workbook. They will be used again in Assignments 3A and 3B.

ASSIGNMENT 3A NUMERIC FILING, CARDS 1–32

Jacobsen's Department Store keeps a separate numeric card file on all credit customers. The numeric card file is organized according to the four-digit customer numbers. It serves as a reference when the customer number is known but the name of the customer is not known. In this assignment, you will practice *numeric* filing with cards 1 through 32. Follow these instructions:

1. *Assemble your materials.* Retrieve the 32 cards used in Assignments 1 and 2 from the pocket in the back of this workbook. Using the number in the upper-right corner of each card, arrange them in order from 1 through 32.
2. *Set up FanFile*. Place *FanFile* in front of you so that Side 1 is facing you. Note that each pocket has a numeric caption at the right for numeric filing: 0000-0999, 1000-1999, 2000-2999, 3000-3999, and 4000-4999. The caption *0000-0999* means that numbers from 0000 through 0999 are filed in numeric order under that caption. The other four captions have the same meaning for their range of numbers. For this assignment, you will file the cards in numeric order in each of the five pockets.
3. *Do a rough numeric sort*. Sort the 32 cards into five stacks according to the first digit of the four-digit account number. You will have stacks for 0, 1, 2, 3, and 4.

4. *File numerically*. Working with one stack at a time, file each card in numeric order in the appropriate pocket of *FanFile*. File each card to the left of the caption so the caption remains visible. For example:

Card 3 with customer number 0793 is filed in the 0000-0999 pocket to the left of the 0000-0999 caption as shown here.

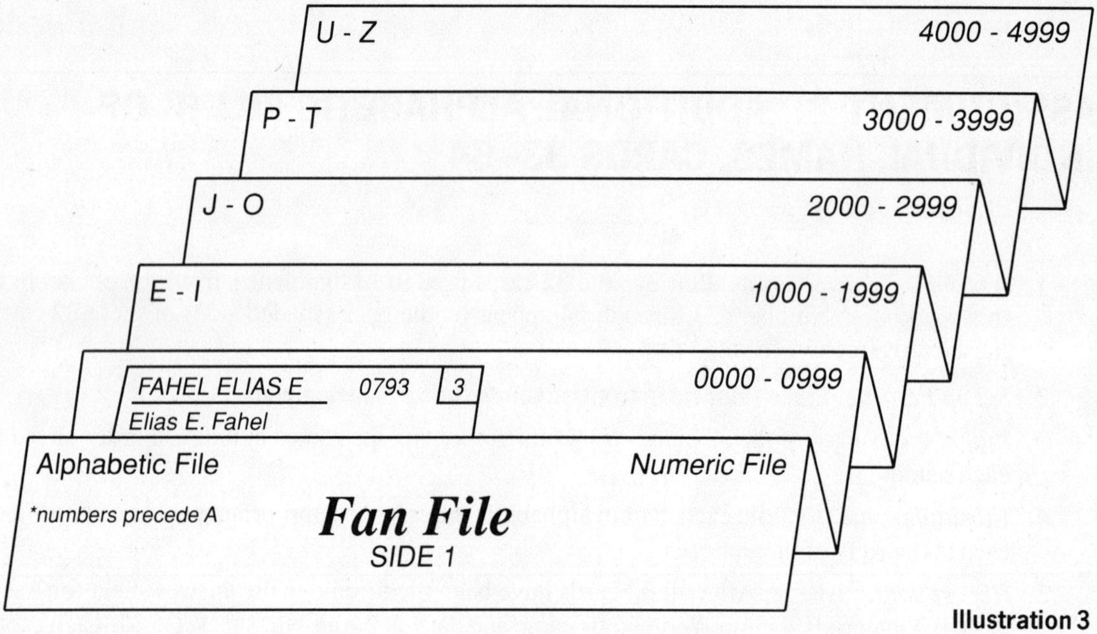

Illustration 3

Card 5 with customer number 0891 is also filed in the 0000-0999 pocket **behind** Card 3, because 0891 comes after 0793.

5. *Report your answers*. After all 32 cards have been filed, remove the answer sheet for Assignment 3A from the materials section. Write your name and the date on the answer sheet. Beside each caption on the answer sheet, list the card number of each card in the order in which it is arranged in the pocket. Report the card number that is in the box at the upper-right corner of each card, not the four-digit customer number. As an example, all of the numbers for the 0000-0999 caption are listed on the answer sheet for you. Be sure that your answers are the same as the example.

6. *Conclude Assignment 3A.* Hand in the answer sheet to your instructor. Remove the 32 cards from the five pockets of *FanFile.* Store them in the pocket in the back of this workbook. They will be used again in Assignment 3B.

ASSIGNMENT 3B ADDITIONAL NUMERIC FILING, CARDS 33–64

1. *Assemble your materials.* Retrieve the 32 cards used in Assignment 3A from the pocket in the back of this workbook. Numbers 33 through 64 appear on the back of these 32 cards. Arrange these cards in order from 33 through 64.

2. *Set up FanFile*. Place *FanFile* in front of you so that Side 1 is facing you. For this assignment, use cards 33 through 64 and the answer sheet for Assignment 3B.

3. *Do a rough numeric sort*. Sort the 32 cards into five stacks according to the first digit of the four-digit account number. You will have stacks for 0, 1, 2, 3, and 4.

4. *File numerically*. Working with one stack at a time, file each card in numeric order in the appropriate pocket of *FanFile*. File each card to the left of the caption so the caption remains visible.
5. *Report your answers*. After all 32 cards have been filed, remove the answer sheet for Assignment 3B from this book. Fill in your name and the date. Beside each caption on the answer sheet, list the card number of each card in the order in which it is arranged in the pocket. Report the card number that is in the box at the upper-right corner of each card.
6. *Conclude Assignment 3B*. Hand in the answer sheet to your instructor. Remove the 32 cards from the five pockets of *FanFile*. With your instructor's consent, discard them or deposit them for recycling. This concludes your manual filing practice with Jacobsen's Department Store. You will do electronic filing for Jacobsen's in Project 3.

ASSIGNMENT 4 ALPHABETIC FILING OF BUSINESS AND ORGANIZATION NAMES, CARDS 65–96

You have secured a position as a new employee in the offices of Fidelity Underwriters, Inc. of Los Angeles, California. Your new employer handles the employee group insurance plans for a number of businesses, organizations, and government agencies. Fidelity's clients are located in five geographic regions of the United States. Your first assignment is to file client records alphabetically according to Filing Rules 6 through 12.

For this assignment, you will use cards that have the numbers 65 through 96 in the upper-right corner. Follow these steps:

1. *Set up FanFile*. Place *FanFile* in front of you so that Side 1 is facing you. For this assignment, you will use the alphabetic captions at the left as you did in Assignments 1 and 2.
2. *Detach sheets with cards 65–96*. Remove the two sheets from the materials section of this workbook that have cards with the numbers 65 through 96 in the upper-right corner. Do not separate the individual cards yet.
3. *Review*. If you are familiar with Filing Rules 6 through 12, proceed to the next step. If not, review Rules 6 through 12 in your textbook (Chapter 5) or on pages 21 through 24 of this workbook.
4. *Organize your materials*. Place the two sheets that you removed from this workbook in front of you. Card numbers 65 through 80 on the first sheet and cards 81 through 96 on the second sheet should be facing up. Ignore the cards on the backs of the two sheets. They will be used in Assignment 5.
5. *Index*. Index each of the 32 names by writing or keying the names in indexed order on the line above each name. The first name has been indexed for you as an example. Remember to use all capital letters and to omit any punctuation.
6. *Separate* the 32 cards at the perforations. Arrange these cards in order from 65 through 96.
7. *File alphabetically*. File each card in alphabetic order in the appropriate pocket of *FanFile*. If the first indexed unit on a card is a number, such as 4, file the card in numeric order in the A-D pocket before names beginning with A. File each card to the right of its caption. Use the same procedures followed in Assignments 1 and 2.
8. *Report your answers*. After all 32 cards have been filed, remove the answer sheet for Assignment 4 from this book. Write your name and the date on the answer sheet. Beside each caption on the answer sheet, list the card number of each card in the order in which it is arranged in the pocket.

9. *Conclude Assignment 4.* Hand in the answer sheet to your instructor. Remove the 32 cards from the five pockets of *FanFile.* Store them in the pocket in the back of this workbook. They will be used again in Assignment 5.

ASSIGNMENT 5 ADDITIONAL ALPHABETIC FILING OF BUSINESS AND ORGANIZATION NAMES, CARDS 97–128

1. *Assemble your materials.* Retrieve the 32 cards used in Assignment 4 from the pocket in the back of this workbook. Numbers 97 through 128 appear on the back of these 32 cards. Arrange these cards in order from 97 through 128.
2. *Set up FanFile.* Place *FanFile* in front of you so Side 1 is facing you. Use the alphabetic captions.
3. *Index.* Index each of the 32 names as you did in Assignment 4.
4. *File alphabetically.* File each card in alphabetic order in the appropriate pocket of *FanFile.* File each card to the right of its caption.
5. *Report your answers.* After all 32 cards have been filed, remove the answer sheet for Assignment 5 from this book. Fill in your name and the date, and beside each caption list the card number of each card in the order in which it is arranged in the pocket.
6. *Conclude Assignment 5.* Hand in the answer sheet to your instructor. Remove the 32 cards from the five pockets of *FanFile.* Store them in the pocket in the back of the workbook. They will be used again in Assignments 6A and 6B.

ASSIGNMENT 6A GEOGRAPHIC FILING, CARDS 65–96

Fidelity Underwriters, Inc. keeps a separate geographic card file on all clients. The geographic card file is organized according to five geographic regions of the United States. The geographic card file is helpful in generating mailings and other activities conducted by each region. In this assignment, you will practice geographic filing with cards 65 through 96. Follow these instructions:

1. *Assemble your materials.* Retrieve the 32 cards used in Assignments 4 and 5 from the pocket in the back of this workbook. Arrange these cards in order from 65 through 96.
2. *Set up FanFile.* Place *FanFile* in front of you so that Side 2 is facing you. Note that each pocket has a geographic caption at the right for geographic filing: NC (North Central) Region, NE (Northeast) Region, NW (Northwest) Region, SC (South Central) Region, and SE (Southeast) Region. You will file the cards for this assignment in geographic order in the five pockets.
3. *Do a rough geographic sort.* Sort the 32 cards into five stacks according to region. On each card, a two-letter region abbreviation is located to the right of the line. You will have stacks for NC, NE, NW, SC, and SE.

4. *File geographically*. Working with one stack at a time, file each card in geographic order in the appropriate pocket of *FanFile*. Within each region, file the cards alphabetically by the two-letter state abbreviation as the abbreviation is written. If both the region and the state are the same, file cards alphabetically by the name of the city. If region, state, and city are the same, file cards alphabetically by business or organization name. For example: cards 65, 75, and 96 are all filed in the NC (North Central) region to the left of the caption. Card 75 (IA) is filed **in front of** card 96 (IL) because *A* comes before *L*. Card 96 is filed **in front of** card 65 (NE) because *I* comes before *N*.
5. *Report your answers*. After all 32 cards have been filed, retrieve the answer sheet for Assignment 6A. Fill in your name and the date, and beside each caption on the answer sheet, list the card number of each card in the order in which it is arranged in the pocket. Report the card number that is in the box at the upper-right corner of each card. As an example, the first number for the NC Region is listed on the answer sheet for you.
6. *Conclude Assignment 6A*. Hand in the answer sheet to your instructor. Remove the 32 cards from the five pockets of *FanFile*. Store them in the pocket in the back of this workbook. They will be used again in Assignment 6B.

ASSIGNMENT 6B ADDITIONAL GEOGRAPHIC FILING, CARDS 97–128

1. *Assemble your materials*. Retrieve the 32 cards used in Assignment 6A from the pocket in the back of this workbook. Arrange these cards in order from 97 through 128.
2. *Set up FanFile*. Place *FanFile* so Side 2 faces you. For this assignment, use cards 97 through 128 and the answer sheet for Assignment 6B.
3. *Do a rough geographic sort*. Sort the 32 cards into five stacks according to region.
4. *File geographically*. Working with one stack at a time, file each card in geographic order in the appropriate pocket of *FanFile*. Within each region, file the cards alphabetically by the two-letter state abbreviation.
5. *Report your answers*. After all 32 cards have been filed, retrieve the answer sheet for Assignment 6B. Fill in your name and the date, and beside each caption on the answer sheet, list the card number of each card in the order in which it is arranged in the pocket.
6. *Conclude Assignment 6B*. Hand in the answer sheet to your instructor. Remove the 32 cards from the five pockets of *FanFile*. With your instructor's consent, discard them or deposit them for recycling. This concludes your manual filing practice with Fidelity Underwriters, Inc. You will do electronic filing for Fidelity in Project 4.

ASSIGNMENT 7A SUBJECT FILING, CARDS 129–160

You have been hired to manage the inventory records at New Age Office Supply. The company is a retail business that sells five basic categories of office furniture, equipment, and supplies. Because inventory records refer to things or items rather than people or businesses, you will file the inventory records by subject. In the subject system used by New Age, a product code is assigned to every type of item in inventory. The product code begins with a letter of the alphabet—*A, B, C, D,* and *E*— for each of the five major product lines. The rest of the product code is numeric. A typical product code looks like this: E1-0245.

For this assignment, you will use cards that have the numbers 129 through 160 in the upper-right corner. Follow these steps:

1. *Set up FanFile.* Place *FanFile* in front of you so that Side 2 is facing you. For this assignment, you will use the subject captions on the left side of the pocket. These subject captions identify each of New Age's major product lines: A—Furniture, B—File Cabinets, C—Accessories, D—Visible Files, and E—Carriers. For this assignment, you will sort the cards into product lines by using the first *letter* of the product code. Then, within each product line, you will file the cards in numeric order using the *numbers* of the product code.
2. *Detach sheets with cards 129–160.* Remove the two sheets from the materials section of this workbook that have cards with the numbers 129 through 160 in the upper-right corner.
3. *Separate* the 32 cards at the perforations.
4. *Do a rough sort.* Sort the 32 cards into five stacks according to the letter at the beginning of each product code. You will have stacks for *A, B, C, D,* and *E*.
5. *File by product code.* Working with one stack at a time, file each card in numeric order in the appropriate pocket of *FanFile*. File each card to the right of its caption. Within a pocket, file cards in numeric order, using the five digits in the product code. Ignore the hyphen in the product number. For example, card 136 with product code D1-0284 is filed in the D—Visible Files pocket **in front of** Card 132 because D1-0284 comes before D1-0333. Card 147 with product code D1-0425 is filed in front of card 156 (D2-0147) because D1 comes before D2.
6. *Report your answers.* After all 32 cards have been filed, remove the answer sheet for Assignment 7A from the materials section of this workbook. Fill in your name and the date, and beside each caption list the number of each card in the order in which it is arranged in the pocket.
7. *Conclude Assignment 7A.* Hand in the answer sheet to your instructor. Remove the 32 cards from the five pockets of *FanFile*. Store them in the pocket in the back of this workbook. They will be used again in Assignment 7B.

ASSIGNMENT 7B ADDITIONAL SUBJECT FILING, CARDS 161–192

1. *Assemble your materials.* Retrieve the 32 cards used in Assignment 7A from the pocket in the back of this workbook. Numbers 161 through 192 appear on the back of these 32 cards. Arrange the cards in order from 161 through 192.
2. *Set up FanFile.* Place *FanFile* in front of you so that Side 2 faces you.
3. *Do a rough sort.* Sort the 32 cards into five stacks according to the letter at the beginning of each product code.
4. *File by product code.* Working with only one stack at a time, file each card in numeric order in the appropriate pocket of *FanFile*. File each card to the right of its caption.
5. *Report your answers.* After all 32 cards have been filed, retrieve the answer sheet for Assignment 7B. Fill in your name and the date, and beside each caption list the number of each card in the order in which it is arranged in the pocket.

6. *Conclude Assignment 7B*. Hand in the answer sheet to your instructor. Remove the 32 cards from the five pockets of *FanFile*. With your instructor's consent, discard them or deposit them for recycling. This concludes your manual filing practice with New Age Office Supplies. You will do electronic filing for New Age in Project 5.

ASSIGNMENT 8 PROJECT QUIZ

Your instructor will give you the Project Quiz for Project 1—Card Filing. Use the answer sheet for Assignment 8 to record your answers to the Project Quiz.

PROJECT TWO

CORRESPONDENCE FILING

You have been hired by Scorcher Athletics, Inc. as their filing administrator. Your major duty is to manage incoming and outgoing correspondence. You are a new employee, so the following information is part of your orientation to the company.

Scorcher Athletics, Inc. is located in Boston, Massachusetts. It produces sportswear and athletic shoes. Scorcher buys leather materials from Regal Leathers in Boston. Scorcher also buys nylon fabric materials and some sportswear designs from Tough-Tear Nylon Company in Cambridge, Massachusetts. Scorcher has a contract with Reggie's Trucking Company in Boston. Reggie's delivers the materials that Scorcher buys to one of its fabricating contractors, Sportswear Sewing Center. The people at Sportswear sew or assemble the materials according to Scorcher's designs. After the products are constructed, several retail stores, such as Sports & Weights Unlimited in Cambridge, purchase the new stock to sell to consumers.

In the past few months, Scorcher has been developing a new running shoe design. It has been enthusiastically supported by the president of the company, Ahmal Jackson. The new design was formally approved by Scorcher in early July (last month). Roxanne Knight is Scorcher's vice president for production and is in charge of implementing the manufacturing of the new line of running shoes.

Regal Leathers has been conducting leather treatment tests to develop chemicals that are more environmentally safe than those now used, and they have been successful. The new chemical treatment, which actually improves the characteristics of the leather, received federal approval on July 25. The people at Regal Leathers believe Scorcher should try the new leather treatment on their new running shoes. Regal suggests that Scorcher introduce this new product as the *Envirun* shoe. Regal Leathers will produce the new treated leather at their Milford facility instead of their Newton plant, which will require some rerouting for the trucking services.

Meanwhile, Tough-Tear Nylon Company has developed a new line of sportswear that coordinates with the design of Scorcher's new *Envirun* shoe. One of Scorcher's best customers, Sports & Weights Unlimited, has begun to prepare their store for this *Envirun* line of sportswear.

ASSIGNMENT 9A MANAGING INCOMING AND OUTGOING CORRESPONDENCE, ITEMS 1–12

In Assignments 9 through 11, you will manage 24 items of correspondence for Scorcher Athletics, Inc. Some of these items of correspondence are incoming whereas others are outgoing. Each item of correspondence has a number in its upper-right corner. This number is for identification purposes only and is not part of the records.

For Assignment 9A, you will deal with the first 12 items of correspondence. You will screen each item, decide what action to take, and then file it alphabetically according to the name of the business to which it was sent or from which it was received.

1. *Detach and examine sheets containing correspondence items 1–12.* Remove correspondence items 1 through 12 from the materials section of this workbook. Correspondence on the **Scorcher Athletics, Inc.** letterhead is a copy of outgoing correspondence. Correspondence on **all other letterhead** is **incoming**—either an original copy or a faxed copy.

2. *Separate* the 12 items of correspondence at the perforations. Beginning with correspondence identified as number 1, arrange the correspondence in numeric order.

3. *Detach and examine the answer sheet.* Retrieve the answer sheet for Assignment 9A. Fill in your name and the date. Notice the headings on the answer sheet: **Item No., Discard? (Yes or No), Alphabetic Caption,** and **Action.**

4. *Screen the correspondence.* Look at each item of correspondence to determine whether it should be kept or discarded according to the following guidelines:

   a. Outgoing correspondence—all copies of outgoing correspondence, that is, correspondence on Scorcher letterhead, should be kept. The fact that a copy was made means it was important enough to be kept and filed. Therefore, write an *X* under **No** in the **Discard?** column of your answer sheet. Place the item face down in a stack of correspondence to be kept.

   b. Incoming correspondence—if incoming correspondence is important to the operations of the business, it should be kept; if it is not, then it should be discarded. Correspondence that relates to accounts payable or accounts receivable, marketing and advertising, shipping and transportation, and design or specifications of products is important to the operations of the business and should be kept. Therefore, write an *X* under **No** in the **Discard?** column of your answer sheet. Place the item on the stack for correspondence to be kept.

      Correspondence about unsolicited merchandise and credit services and routine announcements about business closings and employees should not be kept. Therefore, write an *X* under **Yes** in the **Discard?** column of your answer sheet. Place the item in a stack for correspondence to be discarded.

   c. After screening the 12 items, check to be sure than an *X* has been written under either **Yes** or **No** in the **Discard?** column of your answer sheet for all 12 items.

   d. Put the items to be discarded in the pocket at the back of this workbook. Do not throw away these items until you are instructed to do so.

   e. Place the stack of items to be kept in front of you. The lowest-numbered item should be on top.

5. *Determine the Alphabetic Caption.* All items of correspondence will be filed by a business name.

   a. Select the caption under which each item of correspondence will be filed:

      1. Incoming correspondence—use the business name in the letterhead.

      2. Outgoing correspondence—use the business name that appears in the inside address. Do not use the name of the employee who is sending or receiving the item.

   b. Draw a line under the complete name of the business chosen as the caption under which the correspondence will be filed.

   c. On the answer sheet, write the name of the business chosen for the alphabetic filing caption. The first caption has been entered for you on the answer sheet as an example. For discarded items, no alphabetic caption should be entered on the answer sheet.

d. After completing all the items in the stack, check to be sure that an alphabetic caption has been written on the answer sheet for all items except those to be discarded.

6. *Process the correspondence.* Read each item of correspondence to be kept. Determine what action is to be taken with the item. Write the action at the upper-left corner of the correspondence and in the **Action** column of the answer sheet. Some items of correspondence will have more than one action. Action choices are:

   File: The action for all copies of outgoing correspondence is **file.**

   Route to president: The action for any incoming items addressed to Ahmal Jackson is **route to president.**

   Route to vice president: The action for any incoming items addressed to Roxanne Knight is **route to vice president.**

   Cross-reference: The action for any item you are instructed to cross-reference is **cross-reference.** For your practice, only items 8 and 21 will be cross-referenced although it is possible that in an actual situation, others also would be cross-referenced. On item 8, draw a line under Regal Leathers in the body of the letter and write an *X* to the right of the end of the line. The X indicates that the underlined name will be a cross-reference caption. Write *File and cross-reference* in the upper-left corner of the letter and in the **Action** column of the answer sheet. Remove a cross-reference sheet from the materials section of this workbook and fill it in as follows:

   a. Beside **Name** at the top of the sheet, write *Regal Leathers*.

   b. Beside **File No.** at the top of the sheet, write *8X*.

   c. Beside **Regarding**, write *Transporting new products*.

   d. Beside **Date**, write the date of the item, *8/8/--*.

   e. Beside **Name** under SEE: (on the lower part of the sheet), write *Reggie's Trucking Company*.

   f. Beside **File No.** on the lower part of the sheet, write the item number, *8*.

   g. Place the cross-reference sheet with your stack of correspondence.

7. *Conclude Assignment 9A.* Hand in the answer sheet to your instructor. Store the items of correspondence in the pocket in the back of this workbook. They will be used again in Assignments 10 and and 11.

ASSIGNMENT 9B MANAGING INCOMING AND OUTGOING CORRESPONDENCE, ITEMS 13–24

1. *Detach sheets containing correspondence items 13–24.* Remove correspondence items 13 through 24 from the materials section of this workbook.
2. *Separate the 12 items of correspondence at the perforations.* Beginning with item 13, arrange the correspondence in numeric order.
3. *Detach the answer sheet.* Retrieve the answer sheet for Assignment 9B. Fill in your name and the date.
4. *Screen the correspondence* as you did in Assignment 9A (Step 4).
5. *Determine the alphabetic caption of the correspondence* you decided to keep, and follow the steps in Assignment 9A (Step 5).
6. *Process the correspondence.* Process the correspondence as you did in Assignment 9A (Step 6). For item 21, prepare a cross-reference sheet. The cross-reference caption is REGAL LEATHERS. In the **Action** column of your answer sheet and in the upper-left corner of item 21, write *Route to vice president, cross-reference,* and *file*.

7. *Conclude Assignment 9B*. Hand in the answer sheet to your instructor. Store the items of correspondence in the pocket in the back of the workbook. They will be used again in Assignments 10 and 11.

ASSIGNMENT 10 ALPHABETIC FILING OF CORRESPONDENCE

In this assignment, you will simulate the filing of items of correspondence used in Assignments 9A and 9B. You can assume that they have been acted upon and are ready to be filed. Before you begin, check to see that you have indicated on the answer sheet the correct items for discard. Items that should have been marked for discard are numbers 3 and 4 in Assignment 9A and numbers 22 and 23 in Assignment 9B. For this assignment, you will use the 20 items other than the four that should have been discarded. You will also use the two cross-reference sheets prepared in Assignments 9A and 9B. Follow these steps in simulating the filing of the 20 items and two cross-reference sheets.

1. *Organize your materials*. Arrange the 20 items of correspondence in numerical order according to the identification number in the upper-right corner. Place the items in front of you with the lowest-numbered item on top. Cross-reference sheets 8X and 21X follow items 8 and 21, respectively.
2. *Sort alphabetically*. Sort the items into separate stacks according to the name of the company that was underscored in Assignments 9A and 9B. For cross-reference sheets, use the name at the top of the sheet. You will have a stack for Regal Leathers and other stacks for the other captions.
3. *Arrange chronologically*. Arrange each of the stacks by date, or chronologically. Correspondence is filed in folders with the most recent date in front. Thus, each stack should have the most recent item on top and the oldest item on the bottom.
4. *Detach the answer sheet*. Remove the answer sheet for Assignment 10 from the materials section of this workbook. Write your name and the date on the answer sheet.
5. *File alphabetically*. Simulate filing the items by writing the number of each item beside its caption on the answer sheet. The first item has been recorded on the answer sheet as an example. Be sure that the number for the item with the most recent date is listed first. That number should be followed by the numbers of other items in chronological order to the oldest. Report the cross-reference sheets as numbers 8X and 21X.
6. *Conclude Assignment 10.* Hand in the answer sheet to your instructor. Discard the two cross-reference sheets. Store the items of correspondence in the pocket in the back of this workbook. They will be used again in Assignment 11.

ASSIGNMENT 11 SUBJECT FILING OF CORRESPONDENCE

In this assignment, you will again simulate the filing of the items of correspondence used in Assignment 10. This time you will file the items by subject. For this assignment, you will again use only the 20 items that were kept. Follow these steps in simulating the filing of the 20 items by subject:

1. *Organize your materials*. Arrange the items of correspondence in numerical order according to the identification number in the upper-right corner. Place the items in front of you with the lowest-numbered item on top.

2. *Code by subject.* Read each item of correspondence and determine which of the following subject captions best fits the topic of that correspondence. Write the subject caption in the upper-right corner of the item. Subject caption choices are:

   Accounts Payable: The subject caption for items related to **amounts owed by Scorcher** to its suppliers.

   Accounts Receivable: The subject caption for items related to **amounts owed to Scorcher** by its customers.

   Marketing and Advertising: The subject caption for items dealing with the sale and promotion of Scorcher products.

   Specifications: The subject caption for items having to do with manufacturing requirements, materials, and designs for Scorcher products.

   Transportation: The subject caption for items related to shipping, routes, and delivery of products to or from Scorcher and its contractors.

3. *Sort by subject.* Sort the items into separate stacks according to the subject filing captions that were written in Step 2. You will have five stacks—one for each of the subject captions listed above.
4. *Arrange chronologically.* Arrange each of the stacks by date, or chronologically. Correspondence filed by subject at Scorcher Athletics is organized in folders with the most recent date in front, so each stack should have the most recent item on top and the oldest item on the bottom. Do not arrange the items alphabetically by business name.
5. *Detach the answer sheet.* Remove the answer sheet for Assignment 11 from the materials section of this workbook. Write your name and the date on the answer sheet.
6. *File by subject.* Simulate filing the items by writing the number of each item beside its caption on the answer sheet. The first item has been recorded on the answer sheet as an example. Be sure that the number for the item with the most recent date is listed first. That number should be followed by the numbers of other items in chronological order to the oldest.
7. *Conclude Assignment 11.* Hand in the answer sheet and correspondence items 20 and 21 to your instructor. They will be used in Assignment 12, Project Quiz. With your instructor's consent, discard or deposit for recycling all of the other items of correspondence.

ASSIGNMENT 12 PROJECT QUIZ

Your instructor will give you correspondence items 20 and 21 and the Quiz for Project 2—Correspondence Filing.

Rules for Alphabetic Filing

The 12 rules for alphabetic filing on the following pages are compatible with those adopted by ARMA (the Association of Records Managers and Administrators, Inc.). In order to correctly interpret the rules, you must be able to use four special terms related to alphabetic filing.

Unit. Each part of a name is a unit. The name Teronda Jean Clark has three units: *Teronda, Jean,* and *Clark*. The name *National Rollerblade Manufacturing Company* has four units; *The North Carolina Computer Institute* has five units.

Indexing. Indexing is determining the order and format of the units in a name when alphabetizing. In order to index names, we must know the answer to questions such as these: Is a person's record filed by the first or last name? Is a business record filed under *T* if the name begins with *The*? Is punctuation considered in alphabetizing a name? You will learn the answers to these and other questions about indexing as you study the 12 rules.

Alphabetizing. When you arrange names in alphabetic order, you are alphabetizing them. The names *Bolling, Chou,* and *Diez* are arranged in alphabetic order because *B* comes before *C*, and *C* comes before *D*. The names *Jackson, Jefferson,* and *Jonas* are also arranged in alphabetic order. They each begin with *J*, but the second letter is different. These second letters are in correct alphabetic order; *a* comes before *e* and *e* comes before *o*.

Case. The case of a letter of the alphabet refers to whether it is written as a capital letter *(A)*, called *uppercase,* or as a small letter *(a)*, called *lowercase*. When you alphabetize, it makes no difference whether a letter is written in uppercase or lowercase. Consider an uppercase letter *(H)* to be identical to its lowercase counterpart *(h)*. For example, in filing, the name *McArthur* is considered to be exactly the same as *Mcarthur*.

Alphabetizing Unit by Unit

In the chart below, the names are divided into units. The units are shown in all uppercase letters to emphasize that case is not considered in alphabetizing.

Name	Unit 1	Unit 2	Unit 3
Partyshop	PARTYSHOP		
Pettinger Company	PETTINGER	COMPANY	
Pettinger Manufacturers	PETTINGER	MANUFACTURERS	
Rawls Communications	RAWLS	COMMUNICATIONS	
Rawls Dynasty Computers	RAWLS	DYNASTY	COMPUTERS
Rawls Dynasty Diner	RAWLS	DYNASTY	DINER

The first step in alphabetizing unit by unit is to alphabetize first units. Note the following about the above chart:

1. The names under Unit 1 are in alphabetic order.
2. The name PETTINGER appears twice in the Unit 1 column. If first units are the same, alphabetize second units. In the chart above, note that the names beside *PETTINGER* under Unit 2, *COMPANY* and *MANUFACTURERS*, are in alphabetic order.
3. The name *RAWLS* appears three times in the Unit 1 column. If first *and* second units are the same, alphabetize third units. In the chart above, note that the third units, *COMPUTERS* and *DINER*, determine the alphabetic order of the last two names.

Nothing Comes Before Something. In alphabetizing, an important guideline to remember is *nothing comes before something*. This means that a name such as *Park* comes before a name such as *Parke*. Another example is shown in the chart below.

Name	Unit 1	Unit 2	Unit 3
Kiddytoys	KIDDYTOYS		
Kiddytoys Circus	KIDDYTOYS	CIRCUS	

Note that KIDDYTOYS comes before KIDDYTOYS CIRCUS because nothing comes before something (CIRCUS).

A third example of the *nothing-comes-before-something* principle is shown below.

Name	Unit 1	Unit 2	Unit 3
Millford Rest Stop	MILLFORD	REST	STOP
Millford Restaurant	MILLFORD	RESTAURANT	

In the example above, *Millford Rest Stop* comes before *Millford Restaurant* because REST comes before RESTAURANT.

12 FILING RULES

Rule 1: Names of Individuals

When indexing the name of a person, arrange the units in this order: last name as Unit 1, first name or initial as Unit 2, and middle name or initial as Unit 3. Periods are not used in indexing.

Name	Indexed Name
T. E. Ackerman	ACKERMAN T E
Jamal Rashad	RASHAD JAMAL
Jamal S. Rashad	RASHAD JAMAL S
C. Tyna Sanchez	SANCHEZ C TYNA
Carla Marie Sanchez	SANCHEZ CARLA MARIE

Rule 2: Personal Names with Prefixes

Consider a prefix, such as *Mc* in *McDonald*, as part of the name it precedes. Ignore any apostrophe or space that appears within or after the prefix. Commonly used prefixes are *d', D', de, De, Del, De la, Di, Du, El, Fitz, La, Le, M, Mac, Mc, O', Saint, St., Van, Van de, Van der, Von,* and *Von der*.

Name	Indexed Name
Emma J. De Hart	DEHART EMMA J
Charles Dean MacDowell	MACDOWELL CHARLES DEAN
Phillip O'Day	ODAY PHILLIP
Linda Saint John	SAINTJOHN LINDA
Charlotte L. St.Jean	STJEAN CHARLOTTE L
Ashley VanAllen	VANALLEN ASHLEY
Jenah A. Van Balen	VANBALEN JENAH A

Rule 3: Hyphenated Personal Names

Consider a hyphenated first, middle, or last name as one unit.

Name	Indexed Name
Willard G. Corvin-Rojas	CORVINROJAS WILLARD G
Shawn-Lea Czinzack	CZINZACK SHAWNLEA
Johanna Dejong	DEJONG JOHANNA
Antonio R. Dejong-Valdez	DEJONGVALDEZ ANTONIO R

Rule 4: Abbreviations of Personal Names

Abbreviated and shortened forms of personal names are not spelled out when indexed. For example, *Wm.* is indexed *WM,* not *William. Liz* is indexed *Liz,* not *ELIZABETH.*

Name	Indexed Name
Jos. R. Randolph	RANDOLPH JOS R
Liz Ritchey	RITCHEY LIZ
Billy Dee Rowland	ROWLAND BILLY DEE
Geo. Catlin Rutland	RUTLAND GEO CATLIN

Rule 5: Personal Names with Titles and Suffixes

When used with a person's name, a title or suffix is the last indexing unit used if it is needed to distinguish between two or more identical names. Titles and suffixes are indexed as written, except that periods are not used in indexing.

Titles include *Capt., Dr., Mayor, Miss, Mr., Mrs., Ms.,* and *Senator.* Suffixes include seniority terms (*III, Jr., Sr.*) and professional designations (*CPA, M.D., Ph.D.*).

Name	Indexed Name
Carol King, CPA	KING CAROL CPA
Dr. Carol King	KING CAROL DR
Miss Holly W. Lazar	LAZAR HOLLY W MISS
Mrs. Holly W. Lazar	LAZAR HOLLY W MRS
Daryl E. Mabry, II	MABRY DARYL E II
Daryl E. Mabry, III	MABRY DARYL E III
Daryl E. Mabry, Jr.	MABRY DARYL E JR
Daryl E. Mabry, Sr.	MABRY DARYL E SR
Capt. Lisa R. Martino	MARTINO LISA R CAPT
Lisa R. Martino, CRM	MARTINO LISA R CRM

Rule 6: Names of Businesses and Organizations

Consider the units of business and organization names in the order in which they are normally written. When *The* is the first word of the name, it is indexed as the last unit. Names with prefixes are considered one unit, just as with personal names.

Name	Indexed Name
Allegheny Realty	ALLEGHENY REALTY
Anna Lang Studios	ANNA LANG STUDIOS
The Bank of Vermont	BANK OF VERMONT THE
C H Detective Agency*	C H DETECTIVE AGENCY
CH Detective Agency	CH DETECTIVE AGENCY

CHR Car Rentals	CHR CAR RENTALS
Dymock and Boucher	DYMOCK AND BOUCHER
East Coast Fun Park	EAST COAST FUN PARK
Eastcoasters Bicycles	EASTCOASTERS BICYCLES
El Toro Industries	ELTORO INDUSTRIES
Hospital of Olympia	HOSPITAL OF OLYMPIA
The Jackson Daily News	JACKSON DAILY NEWS THE
Marie Scott High School	MARIE SCOTT HIGH SCHOOL
South East Laundromat	SOUTH EAST LAUNDROMAT
University of Utah	UNIVERSITY OF UTAH

*C H Detective Agency comes before CH Detective Agency because nothing (a blank space between *C* and *H*) comes before something (in this case, the letter *H* after *C*).

Rule 7: Abbreviations in Business and Organization Names

Abbreviations in business and organization names are indexed as written. They are not spelled out. For example, *Inc.* is indexed *INC*, not *INCORPORATED*. Remember, do not include periods.

Name	Indexed Name
Carpets Ltd. of PA	CARPETS LTD OF PA
Data Systems, Inc.	DATA SYSTEMS INC
Dr. Pepper Bottling Co.	DR PEPPER BOTTLING CO
Lt. Penn Equipment Co.	LT PENN EQUIPMENT CO
Ms. Sport Smartwear	MS SPORT SMARTWEAR
N. J. Boothe Agy.	N J BOOTHE AGY
Regal Mfg. Corp.	REGAL MFG CORP

Rule 8: Punctuation in Business and Organization Names

Ignore any punctuation marks that appear in business and organization names. Just as with personal names, hyphenated business and organization names are indexed as one unit. Punctuation marks include the *apostrophe, colon, comma, dash, exclamation point, hyphen, parentheses, period, question mark, quotation marks,* and *semicolon*.

Name	Indexed Name
"Bob" McFall Farms	BOB MCFALL FARMS
Cole-Elliot Used Parts	COLEELLIOT USED PARTS
Economy Rent-a-Car Co.	ECONOMY RENTACAR CO
For Joy! Tenniswear	FOR JOY TENNISWEAR
How's That? Burgers	HOWS THAT BURGERS

Rule 9: Numbers in Business and Organization Names

Arabic numerals (*2, 17*) and Roman numerals (*II, IV*) are considered one unit and are filed in numeric order *before* alphabetic characters. All Arabic numerals *precede* all Roman numerals. Hyphenated numbers (*7-11*) are indexed according to the number before the hyphen (*7*); the number after the hyphen (*11*) is ignored. The letters *st, d,* and *th* following an Arabic numeral are ignored. Thus, *1st* is indexed as *1; 2nd* as *2; 4th* as *4;* and so on.

If a number is spelled out (*First* Street Pizza), it is filed alphabetically as written. Hyphenated numbers that are spelled out (*Twenty-One* Restaurant) are considered one unit (*TWENTYONE* RESTAURANT). An Arabic numeral followed by a hyphen and a word (*7-Gable*) is considered one unit (*7GABLE*).

Name	Indexed Name
7-11 Family Store	7 FAMILY STORE
7 Flags Over Texas	7 FLAGS OVER TEXAS
7th Swan Swimwear Co.	7 SWAN SWIMWEAR CO
11 Pipers Music Shop	11 PIPERS MUSIC SHOP
99 Flavors Yogurt Parlor	99 FLAVORS YOGURT PARLOR
1400 Allendale Apts.	1400 ALLENDALE APTS
Fifty-Fifty Autocars	FIFTYFIFTY AUTOCARS
Forty Mile Steakhouse	FORTY MILE STEAKHOUSE
Four Corners Pharmacy	FOUR CORNERS PHARMACY
Fourth and Main Photo	FOURTH AND MAIN PHOTO
Galen's 6-Way Wrench Co.	GALENS 6WAY WRENCH CO
Galen's Auction Market	GALENS AUCTION MARKET
Wayco 8 Way Carwash	WAYCO 8 WAY CARWASH
The Wayco Eight, Inc.	WAYCO EIGHT INC THE

Rule 10: Symbols in Business and Organization Names

If a symbol is part of a name, the symbol is indexed as if spelled out, as shown here:

Symbol	Indexed As
&	AND
¢	CENT OR CENTS
$	DOLLAR or DOLLARS
#	NUMBER, POUND, or POUNDS
%	PERCENT

Name	Indexed Name
1 # Hamburger Shop	1 POUND HAMBURGER SHOP
58th Street Deli Mart	58 STREET DELI MART
The 58¢ Beef Giant	58CENT BEEF GIANT THE
A & R Appliances	A AND R APPLIANCES
$ Saver Used Appliances	DOLLAR SAVER USED APPLIANCES
# One Cellular Phones	NUMBER ONE CELLULAR PHONES
#1 Amusements	NUMBER1 AMUSEMENTS

Rule 11: Government Names

State and Local Governments

State and local government names are indexed first by the name of the state, county, or city that has immediate jurisdiction over that governmental agency. Therefore, to properly index state and local government names, you have to know whether that agency, board, bureau, or department comes under the state, the county, the township, or the city. For example, a city will have jurisdiction over a board of education, so the city would be indexed first, followed by the board of education.

Name	Under Jurisdiction of	Indexed Name
Board of Education	City	FREEPORT
Freeport, ME		FREEPORT MAINE

Bureau of Weights and Measures Augusta, ME	State	MAINE WEIGHTS AND MEASURES BUREAU OF AUGUSTA MAINE

United States Government Names

United States Government names are indexed first under *United States Government,* then by the department, followed by the bureau or service. In each of the following examples of U.S. Government names, Unit 1 is *United*, Unit 2 is *States*, and Unit 3 is *Government*.

Name	Indexed Name
U.S. Department of Agriculture Forest Service	UNITED STATES GOVERNMENT AGRICULTURE DEPARTMENT OF FOREST SERVICE
U.S. Treasury Department Customs Service	UNITED STATES GOVERNMENT TREASURY DEPARTMENT CUSTOMS SERVICE

Foreign Government Names

Foreign government names are indexed first by the name of the country, then the name of the department, bureau, or board.

Name	Indexed Name
Ministry of Agriculture Tunisia	TUNISIA AGRICULTURE MINISTRY OF
Department of Human Resources Venezuela	VENEZUELA HUMAN RESOURCES DEPARTMENT OF

Rule 12: Addresses

When names are otherwise identical, they may be filed by *address*. The elements of the address are considered in the following order: city, state **(spelled in full)**, street name, quadrant (NE, NW, SE, SW), and house or building number.

Name	Indexed Name
Taco-House 6th Street Dallas, TX	TACOHOUSE DALLAS TEXAS 6 STREET
Taco-House 32 Grantham Avenue Dallas, TX	TACOHOUSE DALLAS TEXAS GRANTHAM AVENUE 32
Taco-House 21840 Grantham Avenue Dallas, TX	TACOHOUSE DALLAS TEXAS GRANTHAM AVENUE 21840
Taco-House 193 Hillary Street Dallas, TX	TACOHOUSE DALLAS TEXAS HILLARY STREET 193

Taco-House 600 Ward St., NE Pierre, SD	TACOHOUSE PIERRE SOUTH DAKOTA WARD STREET NE 600
Taco-House 600 Ward St., SE Pierre, SD	TACOHOUSE PIERRE SOUTH DAKOTA WARD STREET SE 600

MATERIALS FOR FILING PROJECTS

- Filing Cards
- Correspondence Items 1-12
- Cross-Reference Sheets
- Correspondence Items 13-24
- Extra Cross-Reference Sheets
- Answer Sheets, Assignments 1-11

ZOLLER LINDA J	3823	1		2873	9
Linda J. Zoller			Ulrich Paar		
	0891	2		2542	10
Kris D. Ward			A. C. Casteneda		
	0793	3		2805	11
Elias E. Fahel			Chang W. Jung		
	4097	4		1526	12
Sarah E. Fields			Albert Anderson		
	3044	5		1366	13
Marie H. Rojas			German Santos		
	2005	6		3030	14
Marshall G. Johnson, Jr.			Vicky W. Justice		
	4958	7		4148	15
Richard F. Urrutia-Lane			J. M. Gallucci		
	2211	8		3042	16
Tammy Zysman			Kelly R. Von Dohlen		

Heather A. Winkler	1490	**33** Bret L. Arnette	1799	**41**
Michael T. Delafleur	4888	**34** Dr. Kimberly R. Kail	1112	**42**
Diana M. Hackney	0813	**35** Cynthia S. Adams	4073	**43**
Anna K. Vandermeer	2237	**36** Gabriele C. Piermarini	4137	**44**
Jesse Quintero	1379	**37** Thomas M. McCall	1678	**45**
Nancy J. Yaeger	0947	**38** Anne-Marie Grow	3993	**46**
Mary E. Babbitt	0768	**39** Jay C. Underkofler	1616	**47**
Beth-Anne G. Harper	3046	**40** Corazon L. Robera	3472	**48**

J. Gallucci-Grow	2491	17	Douglas G. Farnsworth	0689	25
Capt. Ivory Lewis	2257	18	Luella Kelly	1012	26
Rex M. Blevins	2512	19	Robt. Nelson	0868	27
John Daniel McDonald	1238	20	Jamila Saleh	0882	28
Lorrie P. Gallaway	0932	21	James P. Philipps	1286	29
June M. Epstein	2111	22	M. B. Obrien	2416	30
Henri E. Tohme	4411	23	Melissa Huston	2972	31
Mohamed Gamal-Eldin	4075	24	Elizabeth D. Guynn	3039	32

Verna J. Whetzel	1265	49	Adela Carmen Castenada	3013	57
Mohd-Sidek Abd-Ghafar	0833	50	Matthew E. Vance	4916	58
Gregory T. Cooper	3038	51	Theresa M. D'Orazio	0754	59
Theresa D. Pryzby, MD	3040	52	Johanne J. Fontaine	4753	60
Stephen P. Howard	4612	53	Edith de Leon	0820	61
Lisa A. Luxford	2567	54	Travis Lee-Dugger	4128	62
Capt. K. S. Hong	1711	55	Paige J. Wynne, Jr.	3012	63
Linda R. McDonald	0678	56	Tracy S. Jarrett	4456	64

INTERSTATE MOTELS NC **65**

Interstate Motels
13201 Ramblewood Drive
Lincoln NE 68501–2560

NE **66**

Pier 4 Import Agency
7510 Greengate Drive
Portland ME 04101–0632

NW **67**

Mr. Monro Jeans Mfgrs.
800 Rodeo Circle
Casper WY 82601–2699

SE **68**

Public Data Corporation
PO Box 10001
Miami FL 33155–0001

NE **69**

City of Albany, New York
PO Box 32932
Albany NY 12212–2932

NE **70**

Rockville Steel & Mfg. Co.
PO Box 3246
Pittsburgh PA 15218–3246

SC **71**

Kiddies Kollege Learning Center
4914 Belmont Avenue
Fort Worth TX 76102–2139

SC **72**

Metro-Thermocrete, Inc.
1214 Glenside Drive
Oklahoma City OK 73124–1942

SE **73**

ANA Exterminators, Inc.
PO Box 800
Macon GA 31213–0800

SC **74**

Sun Cycles
PO Box 6400
San Antonio TX 78285–6400

NC **75**

Rowley-Scher Reprographics
209 Franklin Road
Cedar Rapids IA 52401–4871

SE **76**

Randolph Hills Nursing Homes
1640 Marshall Street
Fort Myers FL 33906–0897

SE **77**

Young & Janetis Company
410 Jefferson Street
Roanoke VA 24024–0645

NW **78**

Royce Distributors, Inc.
222 Carousel Lane
Billings MT 59101–6714

NC **79**

Computerpro, Ltd.
5118 Bending Branch Drive
Minneapolis MN 55402–6420

SE **80**

4 by 4 Vehicle Exchange
1415 Opryland Drive
Nashville TN 37205–6281

NW **97**

Rosen's Animal Hospitals
100 Rigsby Street
Medford OR 97501–1670

NE **98**

National Business Lists, Inc.
309 Wilkinson Street
New Haven CT 06512–0954

SE **99**

Watkins Digital Thermometers
2000 Bluegrass Drive
Lexington KY 40513–1418

SC **100**

Penril Data Communications Co.
5855 Deepwater Road
Houston TX 77208–5272

SC **101**

4 Seasons Heating Company
PO Box 1741
Beaumont TX 77704–1741

NW **102**

Sandana Corporation
806 Emmett Drive
Helena MT 59601–0416

SE **103**

IKO Real Estate, Inc.
Route 1, Box 277
Montgomery AL 36120–1240

NE **104**

A #1 Auto Rental
2103 West Main Street
Wilmington DE 19850–0436

NC **105**

Unicorn Galleries
PO Box 7127
Chicago IL 60609–7127

SC **106**

Audiokrafters
8405 Roslyn Avenue
Oklahoma City OK 73126–3524

SE **107**

Gladiator Sports & Awards
9538 Spanish Moss Trace
New Orleans LA 70115–5197

SE **108**

ZS Commercial Signs Company
4800 Berrybrook Drive
Jackson MS 39206–2468

NC **109**

Teletechnics Corporation
PO Box 989
Milwaukee, WI 53202–0989

SC **110**

Vari Comp Systems, Inc.
3801 Orcutt Road
Dallas TX 75262–1460

NW **111**

Samuel C. Boyd & Son, Inc.
2520 Brookwood Road
Portland OR 97208–0745

NW **112**

The Rose Garden Flower Shops
Route 1, Box 424
Olympia WA 98502–0847

SC **81**
L. K. Presley Investment Company
2521 Wildercroft Road
Kansas City MO 64109–5804

SC **82**
The Safemasters Company
PO Box 726
Little Rock AR 72233–0726

NC **83**
Columbus Veterinary Hospital
1708 West Delaware Avenue
Columbus OH 43218–0587

NW **84**
The Datacomm Center, Inc.
PO Box 9027
Vancouver WA 98661–9027

NE **85**
Republic Steel Shelving Co.
4000 Industrial Blvd.
Pittsburgh PA 15220–3464

NE **86**
American Society of Interpreters
2703 Connecticut Avenue
Washington DC 20015–5191

NW **87**
County of Albany, Wyoming
PO Box 1000
Laramie WY 82070–1000

NC **88**
Stereo Sound Service
PO Box 838
Bismarck ND 58501–0838

SC **89**
The Greatest Yogurt on Earth, Inc.
405 West Hilliard Road
Wichita KS 67276–1338

NE **90**
1-Stop Quik Stores
4120 Indian River Drive
Simsbury CT 06070–1031

NC **91**
Silesia Pet Foods
5110 Tomlynn Street
Detroit MI 48234–5505

SE **92**
United Optical, Inc.
6420 Peachtree Street
Atlanta GA 30306–2574

NE **93**
Professional Mgmt. Consultants
3602 Hull Street
Philadelphia PA 19107–4682

NC **94**
Wyrick Engineering, Inc.
3001 Fifth Avenue
Rapid City SD 57701–1064

NE **95**
400 Brands Candy Company
214 Paxton Road
Rochester NY 14692–2151

NC **96**
Quest Systems, Inc.
4200 Michigan Avenue
Chicago IL 60613–3406

SC 113

Perpetual Systems Corporation
237 Lancaster Avenue
Springfield MO 65801–0333

NE 114

DuPont Design Corporation
3220 Goodwin Road
Wilmington DE 19851–0757

SE 115

Pier 901 Food Exports
2007 Coastal Highway
Tampa FL 33630–1141

NC 116

Poly Method Driving Schools
701 Hull Street
Indianapolis IN 46210–2760

NW 117

Pacific Research Corporation
1504 Santa Rosa Road
Seattle WA 98112–3226

NC 118

Wordpro Personnel Services
827 New Glarus Drive
Madison WI 53709–2461

SE 119

Piedmont Investment, Ltd.
3127 Military Road
Norfolk VA 23502–1546

NW 120

1st Bank of California
11501 East Pemberton
Los Angeles CA 90054–6591

SC 121

Luego & Kirk, Ltd.
7727 Gulf Coast Highway
Corpus Christi TX 78410–2154

NE 122

Jewish Community Day Care Centers
PO Box 6343
Syracuse NY 13221–6343

SC 123

Luego and Kirk Medical Centers
7747 Gulf Coast Highway
Corpus Christi TX 78409–6514

NC 124

Fidelity Savings of America
314A North Second Street
Omaha NE 68108–1637

SC 125

Hearn-Kirkwood, Inc.
7420 Alamo Road
San Antonio TX 78214–2716

NW 126

Wilson & Cannon, Inc.
PO Box 1350
Eugene OR 97405–1350

NC 127

O'Brien Mfg. Company
9192 Edwards Street
Wausau WI 54401–1275

SE 128

The Pavilion Hotel
10 Spanish Moss Drive
Savannah GA 31404–2493

129
E1-0245 ULTIMA VINYL ATTACHE
United Luggage
58.24 112.00 16 931.84

130
B3-0398 MOBILE SECURITY CABINET
DCR Business Equipment
212.86 367.00 0 0.00

131
A1-0135 MICROCOMPUTER TABLE
Data Case Enterprises
150.66 279.00 12 1,807.92

132
D1-0333 DATA FILE 3 × 5
Data Case Enterprises
12.25 21.88 16 196.00

133
C1-0385 PHONE LOCK
DCR Business Equipment
4.00 6.35 15 60.00

134
E3-0258 DISK PACK CARRYING CASE
Data Case Enterprises
74.10 142.50 5 370.50

135
A3-0344 PNEUMATIC TASK CHAIR
Steel Furniture Company
68.58 127.00 6 411.48

136
D1-0284 ROTARY CARD FILE 4 × 6
Visual Display Inc.
53.06 94.75 21 1,114.26

137
D2-0157 VISIBLE FRAME 12 × 8
Torrence File Products
14.11 25.20 6 84.66

138
B1-0216 2 DRAWER FILE, LETTER
Steel Furniture Company
98.02 169.00 12 1,176.24

139
E2-0467 CATALOG CASE
Fancini Products
43.16 83.00 2 86.32

140
A2-0188 EXECUTIVE DESK
Steel Furniture Company
463.86 859.00 4 1,855.44

141
D2-0453 VISIBLE FILE 10 TRAY
Torrence File Products
412.72 737.00 0 0.00

142
C1-0153 TELEPHONE LIST FINDER
Superior Office Products
14.30 22.70 18 257.40

143
D1-0124 BUSINESS CARD FILE
Data Case Enterprises
10.05 17.95 68 683.40

144
C2-0398 SHALLOW COIN TRAY
Romero Manufacturing Co.
3.50 5.55 40 140.00

B1-0196 3 DRAWER FILE, LETTER 161
Steel Furniture Company
115.42 199.00 7 807.94

B3-0236 MOBILE PEDESTAL AND FILE 162
DCR Business Equipment
172.84 298.00 4 691.36

D1-0168 DESKTOP VUE FILE 163
Data Case Enterprises
9.07 16.20 13 117.91

E1-0230 PERFECTO LEATHER ATTACHE 164
United Luggage
91.00 175.00 26 2,366.00

B2-0174 4 DRAWER LATERAL FILE 165
Steel Furniture Company
405.86 699.75 27 10,958.22

A1-0157 MICROCOMPUTER STAND 166
Data Case Enterprises
48.06 89.00 6 288.36

E2-0258 SLIM UNDERARM PORTFOLIO 167
Fancini Products
29.48 56.70 15 442.20

B2-0184 3 DRAWER LATERAL FILE 168
Steel Furniture Company
312.01 537.95 12 3,744.12

A2-0315 ADMINISTRATIVE DESK 169
DCR Business Equipment
188.46 349.00 2 376.92

D2-0389 VISIBLE RECORD BOOK 170
Torrence File Products
16.66 29.75 41 683.06

C1-0317 MINI PHONE SHOULDER REST 171
DCR Business Equipment
3.40 5.39 26 88.40

C1-0277 TELEPHONE HEADSET 172
Superior Office Products
18.87 29.95 15 283.05

B3-0189 PRINTOUT MOBILE FILE 173
DCR Business Equipment
126.37 217.88 5 631.85

A3-0279 WORKSTATION CHAIR 174
Steel Furniture Company
57.78 107.00 20 1,155.60

E3-0237 MAG TAPE CARRYING CASE 175
Data Case Enterprises
42.12 81.00 0 0.00

E2-0348 ZIPAROUND PORTFOLIO 176
Fancini Products
54.44 104.70 8 435.52

B2-0194 2 DRAWER LATERAL FILE 145

Steel Furniture Company
242.41 417.95 4 969.64

A2-0299 LATERAL FILE 146

Steel Furniture Company
292.68 542.00 18 5,268.24

D1-0425 CLOSED ROTARY FILE 147

Romero Manufacturing Co.
20.69 36.95 12 248.28

A1-0327 PRINTER STAND 148

Data Case Enterprises
90.45 167.50 7 633.15

A1-0233 BI-LEVEL COMPUTER STAND 149

Steel Furniture Company
83.70 155.00 7 585.90

D2-0463 VISIBLE FILE 17 TRAY 150

Torrence File Products
665.84 1,189.00 0 0.00

B3-0266 DESKTOP FILE 151

DCR Business Equipment
28.71 49.50 18 516.78

C1-0422 MESSAGE HOLDER 152

DCR Business Equipment
2.32 3.69 196 454.72

A3-0256 TASK CHAIR 153

Superior Office Products
72.63 134.50 140 10,168.20

E1-0265 ULTIMA LEATHER ATTACHE 154

United Luggage
111.77 214.95 17 1,900.09

C2-0273 COLOR-KEYED COIN TUBE SET 155

Romero Manufacturing Co.
17.96 28.50 9 161.64

D2-0147 VISIBLE FRAME 12 × 6 156

Torrence File Products
13.27 23.70 8 106.16

B1-0156 5 DRAWER FILE, LETTER 157

Steel Furniture Company
190.82 329.00 18 3,434.76

D1-0137 DESKTOP TRAY FILE 158

Data Case Enterprises
10.36 18.50 55 569.80

C1-0246 TELEPHONE SHOULDER REST 159

Superior Office Products
6.23 9.89 34 211.82

E3-0198 CARTRIDGE CARRYING CASE 160

Data Case Enterprises
41.55 79.90 6 249.30

177
C1-0114 TELEPHONE INDEX
Superior Office Products
13.39 21.25 27 361.53

178
B1-0176 4 DRAWER FILE, LETTER
Steel Furniture Company
137.46 237.00 14 1,924.44

179
A2-0267 CREDENZA
Steel Furniture Company
399.33 739.50 2 798.66

180
C2-0246 CASH DRAWER
Romero Manufacturing Co.
99.86 158.50 3 299.58

181
A1-0359 PAPER FEED TRAY
Steel Furniture Company
18.63 34.50 8 149.04

182
A2-0334 COMPACT DESK
DCR Business Equipment
143.91 266.50 6 863.46

183
E1-0168 RENWAY VINYL ATTACHE
United Luggage
34.06 65.50 30 1,021.80

184
C2-0349 COUNTER CHANGE TRAY
Romero Manufacturing Co.
22.52 35.75 0 0.00

185
D1-0323 DATA FILE 2.25 × 4
Data Case Enterprises
10.63 18.98 6 63.78

186
D1-0225 COVERED SWIVEL FILE
Data Case Enterprises
20.13 35.95 19 382.47

187
C2-0235 CASH BOX
Romero Manufacturing Co.
24.54 38.95 12 294.48

188
C1-0368 PHONE CUSHION
DCR Business Equipment
1.00 1.59 77 77.00

189
C2-0388 DEEP COIN TRAY
Romero Manufacturing Company
5.01 7.95 12 60.12

190
B3-0153 DESK SIDE MOBILE FILE
DCR Business Equipment
74.44 128.35 8 595.52

191
D1-0274 ROTARY CARD FILE 3 × 5
Visual Display Inc.
18.45 32.95 14 258.30

192
A3-0421 ERGONOMIC CHAIR
Steel Furniture Company
194.27 359.75 0 0.00

(1)

Regal Leathers

218 Commonwealth Avenue
Boston, MA 02116-0782

July 28, 19--

Roxanne Knight
Scorcher Athletics, Inc.
374 Quincy Market Road
Boston, MA 02109-1476

Dear Ms. Knight:

Payment is due on Monday, August 14, 19-- for Regular Stock Leather No. 92384 for the month of July.

Description	Quantity	Cost Per Cut Sheet	Total
Reg. Stock Leather No. 92384	200	$90.00	$18,000.00
		Total Payment Due	$18,000.00

Sincerely,

Amy Hart

Amy Hart
Accounts Receivable

tw

(2)

Regal Leathers

218 Commonwealth Avenue
Boston, MA 02116-0782

July 28, 19--

Ahmal Jackson
Scorcher Athletics, Inc.
374 Quincy Market Road
Boston, MA 02109-1476

Dear Mr. Jackson:

I would like to arrange a time, as soon as possible, to display for you some samples of our new treated leather. We can then discuss marketing efforts and information needed for your advertising.

After a year of research and development, Regal Leathers has developed a new leather treatment at the Milford plant that was federally approved on July 25, 19--. This leather treatment is a combination of environmentally safe chemicals that has improved the quality of the leather. Treatment with this new product gives the leather increased softness, flexibility, and durability.

I am suggesting that this new leather treatment be applied to your new running shoe design and that it be introduced as the "Envirun" shoe.

Sincerely,

Laressa Washington

Laressa Washington
Sales Representative

tw

③

Sports & Weights Unlimited
45 University Drive • Cambridge, MA 02138-1318

August 2, 19--

Roxanne Knight
Scorcher Athletics, Inc.
374 Quincy Market Road
Boston, MA 02109-1476

Dear Ms. Knight:

This letter is just a reminder for you that Sports & Weights Unlimited will be closed on Labor Day and will resume business as usual the next day.

Sincerely,

James Black

James Black
Personnel Director

rp

④

SPECIALTY OFFICE SUPPLY COMPANY
6940 NORTH MAIN STREET
MEMPHIS, TN 38112-1704

August 1, 19--

Roxanne Knight
Scorcher Athletics, Inc.
374 Quincy Market Road
Boston, MA 02109-1476

Dear Ms. Knight:

Are you tired of the same old office decor? Then add some variety with our novelty line of office wallpaper, cups, pens, pencils, posters, and calendars. Call now for more information: 1-800-555-5959.

Cordially,

David Wang

David Wang
Sales Representative

gl

(5)

Scorcher
Athletics, Inc.
374 Quincy Market Road
Boston, MA 02109-1476

August 3, 19--

FAX TO: 617-555-3890

Laressa Washington
Sales Representative
Regal Leathers
218 Commonwealth Avenue
Boston, MA 02116-0782

Dear Ms. Washington:

Subject: MARKETING NEW LEATHER TREATMENT

On Monday, August 7, 19-- at 9:00 a.m., I will reserve an hour for your presentation on your new leather treatment. If this new process gives the leather the characteristics you report, I might decide to use it for our new running shoe. We can discuss the details in person on Monday morning.

Sincerely,

Ahmal Jackson

Ahmal Jackson
President

aj

(6)

Scorcher
Athletics, Inc.
374 Quincy Market Road
Boston, MA 02109-1476

August 7, 19--

Frances Choi
Sports & Weights Unlimited
45 University Drive
Cambridge, MA 02138-1318

Dear Frances:

Subject: PAYMENT DUE US

We have not yet received payment for Scorcher products that were shipped to you during the month of June. You should have received our invoice for these products by July 7. Because you have been such a good customer, we will honor our usual 30-day discount policy if we receive your payment by August 14.

Sincerely,

Roxanne Knight

Roxanne Knight
Vice President for Production

rk

(7)

Scorcher
Athletics, Inc.
374 Quincy Market Road
Boston, MA 02109-1476

August 8, 19--

Gary Osborn
Production Director
Regal Leathers
218 Commonwealth Avenue
Boston, MA 02116-0782

Dear Gary:

Subject: LEATHER SPECIFICATIONS

Our president, Ahmal Jackson, has given his approval for the use of your new leather treatment for our new running shoe and for naming this shoe the Envirun shoe. Please propose an amendment to our service contract to include the new leather treatment specifications including costs, stock numbers, terms, and procedures.

Sincerely,

Roxanne Knight

Roxanne Knight
Vice President for Production

rk

(8)

Scorcher
Athletics, Inc.
374 Quincy Market Road
Boston, MA 02109-1476

August 8, 19--

Carmon Ladd
Chief of Shipping
Reggie's Trucking Company
9361 Newbury Street
Boston, MA 02115-1388

Dear Ms. Ladd:

Subject: TRANSPORTING NEW PRODUCTS

Scorcher will be using Regal Leather's new leather treatment made at their Milford, Massachusetts, plant for our new running shoe design called the Envirun shoe. This requires adding another pickup route. Can your company add this new route beginning August 21, 19--, for delivery to Sportswear Sewing Center in Worcester, Massachusetts, with the same pickup times as those previously used for the Newton plant?

Sincerely,

Roxanne Knight

Roxanne Knight
Vice President for Production

rk

(9)

Scorcher
Athletics, Inc.
374 Quincy Market Road
Boston, MA 02109-1476

August 9, 19--

Taylor Johnson, President
Sportswear Sewing Center
2800 Industrial Road
Worcester, MA 02178-1246

Dear Mr. Johnson:

Subject: DESIGN SPECIFICATIONS

I am pleased to inform you about the new leather treatment that has been chosen for our new running shoe design to be called the Envirun shoe. This new leather treatment uses federally approved and environmentally safe chemical compounds, which increase the leather's softness, flexibility, and durability. Scorcher's logo will use the colors of kelly green and medium brown to represent the environmentally conscious product.

Is it possible to have our logo embroidered, rather than glued, onto the shoe? If this can be done, we would like you to do so.

Sincerely,

Ahmal Jackson

Ahmal Jackson
President

aj

(10)

Scorcher
Athletics, Inc.
374 Quincy Market Road
Boston, MA 02109-1476

August 11, 19--

Bruce Richards
Construction Supervisor
Sportswear Sewing Center
2800 Industrial Road
Worcester, MA 02178-1246

Dear Bruce:

Subject: MATERIALS SPECIFICATIONS

We have chosen a new leather treatment for our new running shoe design to be called the Envirun shoe. This new leather treatment uses federally approved and environmentally safe chemical compounds, which increase the leather's softness, flexibility, and durability.

Because of changes in the characteristics of the leather, we have determined that Sportswear Sewing Center should change to thread number 3205 for the Envirun shoe instead of the usual thread number 5698.

Cordially,

Roxanne Knight

Roxanne Knight
Vice President for Production

rk

(11)

Reggie's TRUCKING COMPANY
9361 NEWBURY STREET • BOSTON, MA 02115-1388

August 11, 19--

Roxanne Knight
Scorcher Athletics, Inc.
374 Quincy Market Road
Boston, MA 02109-1476

Dear Ms. Knight:

Yes, Reggie's Trucking Company can add the new pickup route with the same pickup times beginning August 21, 19--. Thank you for continuing to choose Reggie's Trucking Company for your trucking service.

Cordially,

Carmon Ladd

Carmon Ladd
Chief of Shipping

fi

(12)

Scorcher
Athletics, Inc.
374 Quincy Market Road
Boston, MA 02109-1476

August 11, 19--

Bill Shore
Head Dispatcher
Reggie's Trucking Company
9361 Newbury Street
Boston, MA 02115-1388

Dear Bill:

Subject: POSSIBLE TRANSPORTATION DELAYS

This notice is to alert you and the other dispatchers that the new route you will be using to pick up materials at Regal Leathers in Milford, Massachusetts, has a lot of highway construction in progress. The construction is expected to last for at least six months.

Please caution your drivers to allow extra time when traveling this route.

Sincerely,

Roxanne Knight

Roxanne Knight
Vice President for Production

rk

CROSS-REFERENCE SHEET

Name File No. ______

Regarding Date ______________

SEE:

Name File No. ______

CROSS-REFERENCE SHEET

Name File No. ______

Regarding Date ______________

SEE:

Name File No. ______

(13)

Sportswear Sewing Center

2800 Industrial Road

Worcester, MA 02178-1246

August 11, 19--

Ahmal Jackson
Scorcher Athletics, Inc.
374 Quincy Market Road
Boston, MA 02109-1476

Dear Mr. Jackson:

I am delighted to hear about the Envirun shoe and to be doing business with an environmentally conscious organization such as yours.

In response to your request, we can embroider the Scorcher logo onto this shoe. I have told the construction supervisor to include this adjustment in the design specifications.

Sincerely,

Taylor Johnson

Taylor Johnson
President

el

(14)

Tough-Tear Nylon Company

5042 Beacon Street
Cambridge, MA 02138-0814

August 11, 19--

Ahmal Jackson
Scorcher Athletics, Inc.
374 Quincy Market Road
Boston, MA 02109-1476

Dear Mr. Jackson:

Thank you for marketing our latest sportswear design to match your new Envirun shoe line. The enclosed sketches and samples will show you that the clothing style is as equally sleek-looking, comfortable, and durable as the shoe. I believe this design ranks among the best in sportswear fashion.

Please phone me at 555-6237 to give me your reaction to these designs. We will then prepare advertising copy for your approval.

Sincerely,

Tanya Jones

Tanya Jones
Sportswear Designer

Enclosures

tj

(15)

FAX TO: 617-555-8532   FROM: 617-555-9344   10:14 a.m.

Tough-Tear Nylon Company
5042 Beacon Street
Cambridge, MA 02138-0814

August 15, 19--

Ahmal Jackson
Scorcher Athletics, Inc.
374 Quincy Market Road
Boston, MA 02109-1476

Dear Mr. Jackson:

I would like to arrange a time as soon as possible to discuss the coordinated marketing of our new line of sportswear that will match your new Envirun shoe. Please notify me of your earliest available date so we can set up a meeting. Thank you.

Sincerely,

David Kim

David Kim
Sales Representative

dk

(16)

Scorcher
Athletics, Inc.
374 Quincy Market Road
Boston, MA 02109-1476

August 15, 19--

FAX TO: 617-555-9344

David Kim
Sales Representative
Tough-Tear Nylon Company
5042 Beacon Street
Cambridge, MA 02138-0814

Dear Mr. Kim:

Subject: COMBINED MARKETING EFFORT

I will be available to meet with you on Thursday, August 17, at 2:00 p.m., to see your new line of sportswear. If it coordinates well with our new Envirun shoes, we can plan a cooperative marketing effort.

Sincerely,

Ahmal Jackson

Ahmal Jackson
President

aj

(17)

Sportswear Sewing Center

2800 Industrial Road

Worcester, MA 02178-1246

August 14, 19--

Roxanne Knight
Scorcher Athletics, Inc.
374 Quincy Market Road
Boston, MA 02109-1476

Dear Ms. Knight:

Payment is due on Friday, August 25, 19--, for sports shoes numbers 14789, 83498, 68789, and 47929 and for sportswear design numbers S75892, S78589, and S77809 for the time period of August 1 to 15, 19--. Refer to invoices 16-486 and 16-493 for the specific quantities and amounts.

Sincerely,

Maria Sanchez

Maria Sanchez
Accounts Receivable

tw

(18)

Sportswear Sewing Center

2800 Industrial Road

Worcester, MA 02178-1246

August 15, 19--

Roxanne Knight
Scorcher Athletics, Inc.
374 Quincy Market Road
Boston, MA 02109-1476

Dear Ms. Knight:

Thank you for the information about the new leather to be used in your Envirun shoes. As you requested, we will change our specifications to indicate the use of thread number 3205 rather than thread number 5698.

Sincerely,

Bruce Richards

Bruce Richards
Construction Supervisor

rt

(19)

Reggie's TRUCKING COMPANY
9361 NEWBURY STREET • BOSTON, MA 02115-1388

August 16, 19--

Roxanne Knight
Scorcher Athletics, Inc.
374 Quincy Market Road
Boston, MA 02109-1476

Dear Ms. Knight:

I received from Carmon Ladd and Bill Shore your information about the new route that will be needed to pick up materials from the Regal Leathers plant in Milford.

All of our drivers have received the new schedules and directions to the plant, as well as information on precautionary measures they may need to take because of the highway construction.

Cordially,

Todd Franks

Todd Franks
Dispatching Coordinator

tf

(20)

Scorcher
Athletics, Inc.
374 Quincy Market Road
Boston, MA 02109-1476

August 18, 19--

Rhonda Goldberg
Advertising Director
Sports & Weights Unlimited
45 University Drive
Cambridge, MA 02138-1318

Dear Rhonda:

Subject: MARKETING NEW SHOE LINE

Scorcher's new line of running shoes will be ready for your store on October 1. We appreciate your eagerness to help us test market this new product. The line will be called Envirun, and will feature a leather treatment that uses environmentally safe chemical compounds. This innovative treatment was recently developed by Regal Leathers.

In late September, we will send you display posters and ad copy for print advertisements featuring the Envirun shoes. We look forward to receiving sales reports and suggestions for future marketing efforts.

Sincerely,

Roxanne Knight

Roxanne Knight
Vice President for Production

rk

(21)

Sports & Weights Unlimited
45 University Drive • Cambridge, MA 02138-1318

August 23, 19--

Roxanne Knight
Scorcher Athletics, Inc.
374 Quincy Market Road
Boston, MA 02109-1476

Dear Ms. Knight:

Sports & Weights Unlimited will begin an aggressive marketing campaign for your new Envirun line of running shoes starting October 1. If you have sample models available before that time, an advance display could be set up to build customer interest.

Could either you or Regal Leathers send us more information about the environmental aspects of the leather treatment compound? We would like to develop advertising that promotes this feature of the Envirun shoes.

Sincerely,

Rhonda Goldberg

Rhonda Goldberg
Advertising Director

aw

(22)

Tough-Tear
Nylon
Company
5042 Beacon Street
Cambridge, MA 02138-0814

August 24, 19--

Roxanne Knight
Scorcher Athletics, Inc.
374 Quincy Market Road
Boston, MA 02109-1476

Dear Ms. Knight:

The purpose of this letter is to inform you that your previous contact here, Andy Wassman, recently left the company to pursue further education.

I look forward to continuing to work with you.

Cordially,

Rashad Ahmed

Rashad Ahmed
Accounts Receivable

dl

(23)

Sure-Credit, Inc.

P.O. BOX 1535
HACKENSACK, NJ 07606-1535

August 28, 19--

Roxanne Knight
Scorcher Athletics, Inc.
374 Quincy Market Road
Boston, MA 02109-1476

Dear Ms. Knight:

Because of your excellent credit record, Sure-Credit is pleased to inform you that you have pre-approval to receive a $5,000 credit limit with your new credit card from us. This card can be used at many retail stores in Boston and throughout Massachusetts.

The yearly fee for your Sure-Credit is $25, and the annual interest rate for charges not paid within 30 days is 22%. Just complete and return the enclosed form to receive your card.

Sincerely,

Joe Stevens

Joe Stevens
Sales Representative

vm
Enc.

(24)

Tough-Tear Nylon Company

5042 Beacon Street
Cambridge, MA 02138-0814

August 31, 19--

Roxanne Knight
Scorcher Athletics, Inc.
374 Quincy Market Road
Boston, MA 02109-1476

Dear Ms. Knight:

Payment for the materials you received from Tough-Tear during the month of August will be due by September 15. Included are invoice numbers 1692, 1808, 2148, 2212, and 2558.

We appreciate your continued business and prompt payment.

Cordially,

Rashad Ahmed

Rashad Ahmed
Accounts Receivable

dl

CROSS-REFERENCE SHEET

Name File No. ______

Regarding Date ______________

SEE:

Name File No. ______

CROSS-REFERENCE SHEET

Name File No. ______

Regarding Date ______________

SEE:

Name File No. ______

Answer Sheet Name ____________________

Assignment 3A Date ____________________
Numeric Filing

0000 - 0999 25, 3, 27, 28, 2, 21 ____________________

1000 - 1999 ____________________

2000 - 2999 ____________________

3000 - 3999 ____________________

4000 - 4999 ____________________

Answer Sheet Name ____________________

Assignment 1 Date ____________________
Alphabetic Filing
Individual Names

A - D 12, 19, 10 ____________________

E - I ____________________

J - O ____________________

P - T ____________________

U - Z ____________________

Answer Sheet Name ____________________

Assignment 3B Date ____________________
Numeric Filing

0000 - 0999 ____________________

1000 - 1999 ____________________

2000 - 2999 ____________________

3000 - 3999 ____________________

4000 - 4999 ____________________

Answer Sheet Name ____________________

Assignment 2 Date ____________________
Alphabetic Filing
Individual Names

A - D ____________________

E - I ____________________

J - O ____________________

P - T ____________________

U - Z ____________________

Answer Sheet Name ____________________

Assignment 6A
Geographic Filing

Date ____________________

NC REGION 75 ____________________

NE REGION ____________________

NW REGION ____________________

SC REGION ____________________

SE REGION ____________________

Answer Sheet Name ____________________

Assignment 6B
Geographic Filing

Date ____________________

NC REGION ____________________

NE REGION ____________________

NW REGION ____________________

SC REGION ____________________

SE REGION ____________________

Answer Sheet Name ____________________

Assignment 4
Alphabetic Filing
Business Names

Date ____________________

A - D ____________________

E - I ____________________

J - O ____________________

P - T ____________________

U - Z ____________________

Answer Sheet Name ____________________

Assignment 5
Alphabetic Filing
Business Names

Date ____________________

A - D ____________________

E - I ____________________

J - O ____________________

P - T ____________________

U - Z ____________________

Answer Sheet Name ____________________

Assignment 7B Date ____________________
Subject Filing

A—FURNITURE ____________________

B—FILE CABINETS ____________________

C—ACCESSORIES ____________________

D—VISIBLE FILES ____________________

E—CARRIERS ____________________

Answer Sheet Name ____________________

Assignment 7A Date ____________________
Subject Filing

A—FURNITURE ____________________

B—FILE CABINETS ____________________

C—ACCESSORIES ____________________

D—VISIBLE FILES ____________________

E—CARRIERS ____________________

Answer Sheet Name ____________________

Assignment 8 Date ____________________
Project Quiz

Alphabetizing Names of Individuals
6 points each, total 30 points

1. ____________________
2. ____________________
3. ____________________
4. ____________________
5. ____________________

Numeric Filing
5 points each, total 10 points

6. ____________________
7. ____________________

Alphabetizing Business and Organization Names
6 points each, total 30 points

8. ____________________
9. ____________________
10. ____________________
11. ____________________
12. ____________________

Over for questions 13 through 19

Answer Sheet

Assignment 8
Project Quiz (continued)

Geographic Filing
4 points each, total 20 points

13. ____________________

14. ____________________

15. ____________________

16. ____________________

17. ____________________

Subject Filing
5 points each, total 10 points

18. ____

19. ____

Answer Sheet **Assignment 9A: Receipt and Creation of Correspondence**

Name ______________________

Date ______________________

Item No.	Discard?		Alphabetic Caption	Action
	Yes	No		
1		X	Regal Leathers	Route to Vice President; file
2				
3				
4				
5				
6				
7				
8				
9				
10				
11				
12				

Answer Sheet **Assignment 9B: Receipt and Creation of Correspondence**

Name ______________________

Date ______________________

Item No.	Discard?		Alphabetic Caption	Action
	Yes	No		
13				
14				
15				
16				
17				
18				
19				
20				
21				
22				
23				
24				

Answer Sheet Name ______________________

Assignment 10
Alphabetic
Correspondence
Filing

Date ______________________

Regal Leathers 21X ______________________

Reggie's Trucking Company ______________________

Sports & Weights Unlimited ______________________

Sportswear Sewing Center ______________________

Tough-Tear Nylon Company ______________________

Answer Sheet Name ______________________

Assignment 11
Subject
Correspondence
Filing

Date ______________________

Accounts Payable 24 ______________________

Accounts Receivable ______________________

Marketing and Advertising ______________________

Specifications ______________________

Transportation ______________________

INTRODUCTION

DATABASE PROJECTS

A *database* is another name for a group of files that are kept on a computer. An example of a *file* is information about all of the customers of a business. Each item in a file is called a *record*. For example, in a customer file there is one record for each customer. Records contain information that is divided into categories called *fields*. An example of information in a field of a customer's record is *4738,* the customer's account number.

Just as with paper files, if you want to look up information in a database, you first need to know something unique about the record you are looking for. For example, if you are searching for a customer's record, you need to know the customer's name or account number — information that is unique to the customer. Fields that contain unique information are called *key fields*. Every record must have one or more key fields so that a specific record can be found when it is needed.

The first three database projects allow you to work with computer files that have been entered onto the data disk that accompanies this text guide. The fourth project, which challenges you to design and establish a new database for a small firm, will require you to obtain a new, formatted floppy disk. The four projects are:

Project 3: Jacobsen's Department Store
A retail customer file with 200 customer records

Project 4: Fidelity Underwriters, Inc.
A group insurance file with 100 client records

Project 5: New Age Office Supply
A retail inventory file with 200 product records

Project 6: Burger Barn
A personnel file with 30 employee records

At the end of each database project in this text guide, there is a project quiz. Each quiz is based on what you have learned in the project and includes questions that you answer by looking at database information on your computer screen. The quizzes were prepared under the assumption that all assignments prior to the quiz were completed correctly or were corrected. To ensure the accuracy of your database prior to taking the quiz, you can check your data against the printouts that appear at the end of each project. Before taking the first quiz on page 99, you should check the accuracy of your database with the printout on pages 101 to 110.

NAME Robyn Allen
DATE ____
SCORE ____

PROJECT THREE

JACOBSEN'S DEPARTMENT STORE

You will recall working with the records of Jacobsen's Department Store in Project 1. The owners of Jacobsen's have decided to convert their customer records to an electronic database. In this project you will be responsible for managing the database for the 200 credit customers of Jacobsen's.

ASSIGNMENT 13: EXPLORE THE CUSTOMER FILE

Follow your instructor's direction to load the program and data disks. Retrieve the data disk file named PROJECT 3, which is Jacobsen's customer file. Explore the file, and as you do so, answer the following questions.

1. What are the names of the fields? (The first answer is given as an example in Lotus; for dBase and Access it would be ACCOUNT___NO.)

Field Names	Field Names
ACCOUNT #	State
Name	Zip
Indexed Name	Phone
Address	Cr. Limit
City	Cr. Rating.

2. How many digits are in each account number? 2. 4

3. What is the name of the customer whose account number is 1301? Ricka L. Fleschner

4. Each customer's name is entered in the Name field in address, or standard, order and again in the Indexed Name field in indexed order. *Indexed order* means that a person's name has been transposed, written in all-capital letters, and has no punctuation. The purpose of the Indexed Name field is to enable the user to sort names into correct alphabetic order. Find account number 2075. What is the indexed name of this customer? Gamaleldin mohamed

5. What is the address of the customer whose account number is 1192? 20524 Floyd Avenue

6. All of the customers live in Illinois (IL) or Missouri (MO). The customer having account number 3037 lives in which state? **6.** Missouri (MO)

7. The last four digits of the ZIP Code are called the ZIP Code extension. What is the ZIP Code extension of the customer whose account number is 1806? **7.** 1154

8. The first three digits in the Phone field make up the area code. What is the area code of the customer whose account number is 2297? **8.** 314

9. Each customer has a credit limit. The credit limit is the largest balance that a customer's account may have. The lowest credit limit in this customer file is $500, and the limits increase in $250 steps to a maximum credit limit of $2,000. What amount is in the Credit Limit field of the customer whose account number is 3016? **9.** 1750

10. In the Credit Rating field, each customer is given a rating of A, B, or C, depending upon how prompt the customer has been in paying the monthly bill. A rating of A means excellent, B means good, and C means fair. Does the customer whose account number is 2338 have an excellent credit rating? **10.** A

NAME ____________________

DATE ____________________

SCORE ____________________

PROJECT THREE

JACOBSEN'S DEPARTMENT STORE

ASSIGNMENT 14 MAKE CHANGES IN THE CUSTOMER FILE

Following is information needed to make changes in ten customer records. After you have made each change, document it by writing the name (or changed name) of the customer for whom the change was made. The first item is an example for a change that has already been made.

Acct #	Change	Name
0. 2528	Credit limit to $1,000	0. Chang-Hong Wu
1. 0982	Phone to 314-555-8894	1. Ivan Jablonski
2. 2968	Name to Samuel L. Fong and Indexed Name to FONG SAMUEL L	2. Samuel L. Fong
3. 3032	Credit rating to A	3. Dr. Elbert Roberts
4. 2005	Address to 1213 Deerfield Lane and ZIP Code extension to 1609	4. Marshall G. Johnson Jr.
5. 1678	Phone to 314-555-1434	5. Thomas M McCall
6. 1381	Credit limit to $1,500	6. Ann Aikensnye
7. 1892	Address to P.O. Box 1848 and ZIP Code extension to 1848	7. Armando Castaneda
8. 0781	Credit rating to B	8. John MacDonald
9. 2268	Name to Karen H. Krause-Daniels and Indexed Name to KRAUSEDANIELS KAREN H	9. Karen H. Krause
10. 2747	Credit limit to $1,750 and credit rating to B	10. ERIC J Wuchira

NAME ______________________

DATE ______________________

SCORE ______________________

PROJECT THREE

JACOBSEN'S DEPARTMENT STORE

ASSIGNMENT 15 DELETE RECORDS FROM THE CUSTOMER FILE

Five customers have closed their charge accounts with Jacobsen's Department Store. Use the information below to delete the records for them. Document the fact that the deletions have been made by writing your initials in the Account Closed By column.

	# of Account to Be Closed		Account Closed By
1.	2867	**1.**	RA
2.	0725	**2.**	RA
3.	2089	**3.**	RA
4.	1568	**4.**	RA
5.	2311	**5.**	RA

NAME ____________

DATE ____________

SCORE ____________

PROJECT THREE

JACOBSEN'S DEPARTMENT STORE

ASSIGNMENT 16 PRACTICE INDEXING NAMES

One of your responsibilities is to establish records for new customers. Before you enter new records into a customer file, you will need to know how to write the customer names in indexed form so they can be keyed correctly in the Indexed Name field. In this assignment, you will practice writing names of individuals in indexed form. If you are not familiar with the rules for indexing names of individuals, consult Chapter 5 in the textbook *Professional Records Management*.

Remember that indexed names of persons are transposed and keyed in all-capital letters without punctuation. Examples of names and how they are written in indexed form follow.

Name	Indexed Name
Roberta A. Wilson	WILSON ROBERTA A
Patrick M. O'Reilly	OREILLY PATRICK M
Kathy Von der Kellen	VONDERKELLEN KATHY
Huang R. Tsu-Wong	TSUWONG HUANG R
Dr. Hamed D. Rashad	RASHAD HAMED D DR
Elizabeth R. Doss, CPA	DOSS ELIZABETH R CPA

Using the above examples as a guide, write the indexed form of each of the following names.

Name	Indexed Name
1. Martha F. Pinzon	1. PINZON MARTHA F
2. Richard d'Angelo	2. D ANGELO RICHARD
3. Kirsten A. Van Camp	3. VANCAMP KIRSTEN A
4. Warren E. Wise-Lockwood	4. WISELOCKWOOD WARREN E
5. Capt. Gail E. Coffey	5. COFFEY GAIL E CAPT

6. Leslie G. Cinalli, Ph.D. — 6. CINALLI LESLIE G PHD

7. Ann-Marie Donally — 7. DONALLY ANNMARIE

8. Mohamed E. Pavlevi — 8. PAVLEVI MOHAMED E

9. Erin G. McAllister — 9. MCALLISTER ERIN G

10. Dorsey Wardlow, Jr. — 10. WARDLOW DORSEY JR.

195 records.

NAME ____________________

DATE ____________________

SCORE ____________________

PROJECT THREE

JACOBSEN'S DEPARTMENT STORE

ASSIGNMENT 17 ADD RECORDS TO THE CUSTOMER FILE

Ten new customers have opened charge accounts with Jacobsen's. Shown below are forms containing the account number for each new customer; the name, address, and phone number of each; and the credit limit and credit rating that have been assigned by the credit manager. Add the ten new customers to the file. As you do so, it will be up to you to determine the indexed name from the name that is given. Write the indexed name in the space provided on each form.

✓ACCOUNT #: 3038 NAME: Gregory T. Cooper

INDEXED NAME: COOPER GREGORY T

ADDRESS: 801 Ingalls Street CITY: Granite City STATE: IL

ZIP: 62040-1434 PHONE: 618-555-6238 CR. LIMIT: 500 CR. RATING: C

✓ACCOUNT #: 3039 NAME: Elizabeth D. Guynn

INDEXED NAME: GUYNN ELIZABETH D

ADDRESS: 214 Fairfax Street CITY: Ferguson STATE: MO

ZIP: 63135-2413 PHONE: 314-555-7226 CR. LIMIT: 1000 CR. RATING: B

✓ACCOUNT #: 3040 NAME: Theresa D. Pryzby, MD

INDEXED NAME: PRYZBY THERESA D MD

ADDRESS: 375 Clearview Drive CITY: Spanish Lake STATE: MO

ZIP: 63137-1255 PHONE: 314-555-8838 CR. LIMIT: 1500 CR. RATING: A

✓ACCOUNT #: 3041 NAME: Louis Heath-Camp

INDEXED NAME: HEATHCAMP LOUIS

ADDRESS: PO Box 133 CITY: St. Charles STATE: MO

ZIP: 63301-0133 PHONE: 314-555-8292 CR. LIMIT: 750 CR. RATING: B

ACCOUNT #: 3042 NAME: Kelly R. Von Dohlen

INDEXED NAME: VONDOHLEN KELLY R.

ADDRESS: 965 Cardinal Drive CITY: Spanish Lake STATE: MO

ZIP: 63137-1348 PHONE: 314-555-7810 CR. LIMIT: 1000 CR. RATING: B

ACCOUNT #: 3043 NAME: Sean O'Hara

INDEXED NAME: OHARA SEAN

ADDRESS: 2803 Chelsea Court CITY: Alton STATE: IL

ZIP: 62002-3291 PHONE: 618-555-9190 CR. LIMIT: 750 CR. RATING: C

ACCOUNT #: 3044 NAME: Marie H. Rojas

INDEXED NAME: ROJAS MARIE H

ADDRESS: 104 South Fifth Street CITY: Spanish Lake STATE: MO

ZIP: 63137-2558 PHONE: 314-555-8702 CR. LIMIT: 750 CR. RATING: B

ACCOUNT #: 3045 NAME: Dr. Tony V. Estrella

INDEXED NAME: ESTRELLA TONY V DR

ADDRESS: 401 Giles Road CITY: Jennings STATE: MO

ZIP: 63136-0825 PHONE: 314-555-3171 CR. LIMIT: 1500 CR. RATING: B

ACCOUNT #: 3046 NAME: Beth-Anne G. Harper

INDEXED NAME: HARPER BETHANNE G

ADDRESS: Route 2, Box 156 CITY: Spanish Lake STATE: MO

ZIP: 63137-0989 PHONE: 314-555-0830 CR. LIMIT: 1250 CR. RATING: B

ACCOUNT #: 3047 NAME: Stephen L. Wallenstein

INDEXED NAME: WALLENSTEIN STEPHEN L

ADDRESS: 1009 Ascot Lane CITY: St. Louis STATE: MO

ZIP: 63106-5410 PHONE: 314-555-8275 CR. LIMIT: 500 CR. RATING: C

205

NAME ____________

DATE ____________

SCORE ____________

PROJECT THREE

JACOBSEN'S DEPARTMENT STORE

ASSIGNMENT 18 RETRIEVE INFORMATION FROM CUSTOMER RECORDS

You have received requests from the sales manager for the following information about credit customers. Write your response to each request in the column at the right. One example is given.

Information Requested	Response
0. Name of customer with account number 1073	**0.** Cynthia S. Adams
1. Phone number of account number 2652	**1.** 314-555-9469
2. Credit limit of Daniel P. Schlotzhauer 1518	**2.** $1000
3. Phone number of Diego H. Vaccarezza 0840	**3.** 618-555-8747
4. Street address of Lora-Lee Kelley 2273	**4.** 417 Creekview Road
5. Credit limit and credit rating of account number 2195	**5.** B.
6. Name of customer whose phone number is 314-555-8639	**6.** Theresa M. Dorazio
7. Account number of Denise J. Schuster	**7.** 2391
8. Name and full address of account number 2237	**8.** Anna K. Vandermeer 719 Kenneth Drive Spanish Lake, MO 63137-0815

9. Credit rating of Barry D. Lawson

9. C

10. Account number and name of customer whose address is PO Box 909, Spanish Lake, MO

10. 1625
Runtao Yan.

NAME ____________

DATE ____________

SCORE ____________

PROJECT THREE

JACOBSEN'S DEPARTMENT STORE

ASSIGNMENT 19 RETRIEVE INFORMATION FROM THE CUSTOMER FILE

Another of your job responsibilities is to use your customer file to look up requested information about groups of customers. Each of the questions below represents a request about groups of customers that has been given to you.

1. How many customers have a credit rating of C? **1.** 30

2. How many customers have a credit limit of more than $1,500? (Do not include customers whose credit limit is $1,500.) **2.** 32

3. What are the names and phone numbers of all customers who live in St. Charles?

Name	Phone
Minyung Chang	314-555-5665
Henri E. Tohme	314-555-1417
Neva M Turano	314-555-1153
David H. Conhen Jr.	314-555-7066
Nancy E. Parks	314-555-8553
Louis Heath-camp	314-555-8292

4. How many customers live in Illinois? **4.** 25

5. What are the account numbers and names of all customers whose last names begin with the letter F?

Account #	Name
0793	ELIAS E FANNON
1441	CAROLYN C FANNON
0689	DOUGLAS G FARNSWORTH
2097	Sarah E Fields
1301	RICKA L FLESCHNER
1339	SAML T. FONG
2968	SAMUEL L FONG
2753	Johanne J. FONTAINE

6. How many customers have a credit rating of B *and* a credit limit of $1,000? **6.** 59

7. What are the names of the customers who live in St. Louis *and* have a credit limit of $1,750?

Verna J. Whetzel

IVAN JABLONSKI

8. What are the names of customers whose last names begin with the letters G, H, and I *and* who have a credit rating of A? Roberto P. Gregorio, Caroline Hostetter, Paul A IFJU, Christopher L Impellitteri

9. How many customers who live in Florissant have a credit rating of B? **9.** 9

10. How many of our customers who live in Missouri have a credit limit less than $750? (Do not count those whose credit limit is $750.) **10.** 18

H.W. 06/11/01

NAME ____________________

DATE ____________________

SCORE ____________________

PROJECT THREE
JACOBSEN'S DEPARTMENT STORE

ASSIGNMENT 20 PRINT CUSTOMER INFORMATION

The electronic customer file is used by Jacobsen's Department Store for many applications. One very important use is the creation of printed reports, lists, and labels. In this assignment you will use the customer file to respond to requests for printed information. After completing each printing job, answer the question related to it in the space provided.

1a. Print a mailing label for each customer who lives in Alton, IL. Each label should include data from the following fields: Name, Address, City, State, and ZIP. Add USA/ra.

1b. How many labels did you print? query save — **1b.** 9

2a. Print a list of the account numbers, names, and credit limits of all customers with account numbers less than 1000. Print the list in ascending order by account number. You may include headings if your software allows.

query save.

2b. How many customers are on the list? — **2b.** 29

3a. Print an alphabetic list of the names and phone numbers of customers who live in Ferguson, MO. Hint: You may want to do an alphabetic sort on the Indexed Name field, but print the selected names from the Name field.

3b. How many customers are on the list? — **3b.** 12

NAME ____________________

DATE ____________________

SCORE ____________________

PROJECT THREE

JACOBSEN'S DEPARTMENT STORE

ASSIGNMENT 21 PROJECT QUIZ

Before you take this quiz, you should have completed the previous assignments so that your customer file will be completely updated. You will use the customer file at your computer to answer the questions.

1. How many fields are in the customer file for Jacobsen's Department Store? **1.** 10

2a. What is the phone number of the customer whose account number is 0882? **2a.** 314-555-7223

2b. Change this phone number to 314-555-4917. Document the change by writing the name of the customer. **2b.** JS

3a. What is the name of the customer whose account number is 1048? **3a.** Michael S. Salewski

3b. Delete this customer record from the file, and document the deletion by writing your initials. **3b.** RA

4. Add a record to the customer file using the following information. Write the indexed name of the new customer in the space provided.

```
ACCOUNT #:  3048      NAME:  Reva G. Shane-Lewis
INDEXED NAME:  SHANELEWIS REVA G
ADDRESS:  318 Darlington Avenue           CITY:  Spanish Lake     STATE:  MO
ZIP:  63137-1250    PHONE:  314-555-2132    CR. LIMIT:  750    CR. RATING:  B
```

5. What are the credit limit and credit rating of the customer having account number 2290? **5.** $1500 B

6. What is the phone number of Heather A. Winkler? 6. 314-555-4426

7. How many customers live in Edwardsville? 7. 6

8. List the names of all customers who live in Illinois *and* have a credit rating of C. Gregory T. Cooper J.M. Gallucci, Scott M Garber, Sean O'HARA

9. List the names of all customers who have a credit limit less than $750 (does not include $750) *and* a credit rate of C. GREGORY T. COOPER, J M GALLUCCI, GERMAN SANTOS, DR. REBECCA B. REDFERN, CAPT IVORY LEWIS, STEPHEN P HOWARD, STEPHANIE J VILLA, PAIGE J. WYNNE JR, STEPHEN L WALLENSTEIN

(9)

10. Print a mailing label for each customer living in Spanish Lake whose last name begins with the letter *S*. How many labels did you print? Attach the labels to this quiz and give it to your instructor. 10. 8

Project Three (Printout of Database After Completion of All Assignments Except Quiz)

	ACCOUNT #	NAME	INDEXED NAME
1.	0678	Linda R. McDonald	MCDONALD LINDA R
2.	0689	Douglas G. Farnsworth	FARNSWORTH DOUGLAS G
3.	0701	Charlotte O'Bryen	OBRYEN CHARLOTTE
4.	0722	Caroline Hostetter	HOSTETTER CAROLINE
5.	0738	Dina L. Walsh	WALSH DINA L
6.	0745	Harvey Ramirez, Ph.D.	RAMIREZ HARVEY PHD
7.	0752	Tuan Q. Ta	TA TUAN Q
8.	0754	Theresa M. D'Orazio	DORAZIO THERESA M
9.	0768	Mary E. Babbitt	BABBITT MARY E
10.	0781	John MacDonald	MACDONALD JOHN
11.	0793	Elias E. Fahel	FAHEL ELIAS E
12.	0801	Patricia E. Uhlrich	UHLRICH PATRICIA E
13.	0813	Diana M. Hackney	HACKNEY DIANA M
14.	0820	Edith de Leon	DELEON EDITH
15.	0833	Mohd-Sidek Abd-Ghafar	ABDGHAFAR MOHDSIDEK
16.	0840	Diego H. Vaccarezza	VACCAREZZA DIEGO H
17.	0855	Karen C. Cammarota	CAMMAROTA KAREN C
18.	0868	Robt. Nelson	NELSON ROBT
19.	0882	Jamila Saleh	SALEH JAMILA
20.	0891	Kris D. Ward	WARD KRIS D
21.	0911	Alyssa Eckstein	ECKSTEIN ALYSSA
22.	0925	Erin O'Bryant	OBRYANT ERIN
23.	0932	Lorrie P. Gallaway	GALLAWAY LORRIE P
24.	0947	Nancy J. Yaeger	YAEGER NANCY J
25.	0950	Paul A. Ifju	IFJU PAUL A
26.	0961	Kitt Irwin	IRWIN KITT
27.	0978	Scott R. Taulbee	TAULBEE SCOTT R
28.	0982	Ivan Jablonski	JABLONSKI IVAN
29.	0995	Charles G. Zehmer, III	ZEHMER CHARLES G III
30.	1012	Luella Kelly	KELLY LUELLA
31.	1023	Angelina T. Washington	WASHINGTON ANGELINA T
32.	1035	Karen J. DaCosta	DACOSTA KAREN J
33.	1048	Michael S. Salewski	SALEWSKI MICHAEL S
34.	1055	Jesse Quintero, III	QUINTERO JESSE III
35.	1067	Gina L. Barnett	BARNETT GINA L
36.	1073	Cynthia S. Adams	ADAMS CYNTHIA S
37.	1089	Dean M. Umberger	UMBERGER DEAN M
38.	1099	Robert W. Nelson	NELSON ROBERT W
39.	1112	Dr. Kimberly R. Kail	KAIL KIMBERLY R DR
40.	1127	John E. Van Stavoren	VANSTAVOREN JOHN E
41.	1133	Mitchell S. La Barre	LABARRE MITCHELL S
42.	1148	J. M. Gallucci	GALLUCCI J M
43.	1159	Elizabeth T. Webster	WEBSTER ELIZABETH T
44.	1167	Min-Yung Chang	CHANG MINYUNG
45.	1188	Lois M. Thompson	THOMPSON LOIS M
46.	1192	Rose Mary Le Mieux	LEMIEUX ROSE MARY
47.	1205	Raleigh A. Sandy, III	SANDY RALEIGH A III
48.	1216	Jean A. Jackson	JACKSON JEAN A
49.	1228	Scott M. Garber	GARBER SCOTT M
50.	1238	John Daniel McDonald	MCDONALD JOHN DANIEL
51.	1249	Laura A. Hall	HALL LAURA A
52.	1265	Verna J. Whetzel	WHETZEL VERNA J
53.	1272	Ruth S. Machara	MACHARA RUTH S
54.	1286	James P. Philipps	PHILIPPS JAMES P
55.	1301	Ricka L. Fleschner	FLESCHNER RICKA L
56.	1305	Javier Xicontencatl	XICONTENCATL JAVIER

	ACCOUNT #	NAME	INDEXED NAME
57.	1322	John R. Beauchamp	BEAUCHAMP JOHN R
58.	1339	Saml. T. Fong	FONG SAML T
59.	1341	Edward G. Engel	ENGEL EDWARD G
60.	1343	David C. Williamson	WILLIAMSON DAVID C
61.	1366	German Santos	SANTOS GERMAN
62.	1379	Jesse Quintero	QUINTERO JESSE
63.	1381	Ann Aikens-Nye	AIKENSNYE ANN
64.	1402	James Zimmer	ZIMMER JAMES
65.	1411	Henri E. Tohme	TOHME HENRI E
66.	1438	Rev. Harvey Ramirez	RAMIREZ HARVEY REV
67.	1441	Carolyn C. Fannon	FANNON CAROLYN C
68.	1456	Tracy S. Jarrett	JARRETT TRACY S
69.	1466	Michele A. Del Gallo	DELGALLO MICHELE A
70.	1473	L. Irwin	IRWIN L
71.	1490	Heather A. Winkler	WINKLER HEATHER A
72.	1502	Christopher L. Impellitteri	IMPELLITTERI CHRISTOPHER L
73.	1518	Daniel P. Schlotzhauer	SCHLOTZHAUER DANIEL P
74.	1526	Albert Anderson	ANDERSON ALBERT
75.	1539	Kimberly R. Kail, CPA	KAIL KIMBERLY R CPA
76.	1552	Karen A. Saul	SAUL KAREN A
77.	1593	Rebecca B. Redfern, MD	REDFERN REBECCA B MD
78.	1608	Denise L. LaBarre	LABARRE DENISE L
79.	1616	Jay C. Underkofler	UNDERKOFLER JAY C
80.	1625	Run-Tao Yan	YAN RUNTAO
81.	1639	Amy Anderson	ANDERSON AMY
82.	1656	Lisa J. Wong	WONG LISA J
83.	1678	Thomas M. McCall	MCCALL THOMAS M
84.	1693	Nehru B. Essomba	ESSOMBA NEHRU B
85.	1711	Capt. K. S. Hong	HONG K S CAPT
86.	1738	Audrey C. Tsai	TSAI AUDREY C
87.	1746	Cindy Rea D. Johnson	JOHNSON CINDY REA D
88.	1755	W. Randolph Gill	GILL W RANDOLPH
89.	1769	N. B. O'Brien	OBRIEN N B
90.	1772	George S. Savopoulos	SAVOPOULOS GEORGE S
91.	1784	Lucy L. Hanks	HANKS LUCY L
92.	1799	Bret L. Arnette	ARNETTE BRET L
93.	1806	J. Howard Breithaupt	BREITHAUPT J HOWARD
94.	1811	James C. Woods	WOODS JAMES C
95.	1823	Linda J. Zoller	ZOLLER LINDA J
96.	1834	Mark D. Cheslow	CHESLOW MARK D
97.	1856	Dr. Rebecca B. Redfern	REDFERN REBECCA B DR
98.	1868	Wong-Kyou Kim	KIM WONGKYOU
99.	1875	Paul Nguyen	NGUYEN PAUL
100.	1888	Michael T. Delafleur	DELAFLEUR MICHAEL T
101.	1892	Armando Castaneda	CASTANEDA ARMANDO
102.	1905	Deanna E. Pendrey	PENDREY DEANNA E
103.	1916	Matthew E. Vance	VANCE MATTHEW E
104.	1929	Betsy F. Sayre	SAYRE BETSY F
105.	1932	Bonnie J. Neal	NEAL BONNIE J
106.	1940	Fu-Sheng Tsai	TSAI FUSHENG
107.	1949	James H. Woods	WOODS JAMES H
108.	1958	Richard F. Urrutia-Lane	URRUTIALANE RICHARD F
109.	1969	Jas. A. Philipps	PHILIPPS JAS A
110.	1982	E. Steven Ingram	INGRAM E STEVEN
111.	1999	Alec A. Berry	BERRY ALEC A
112.	2005	Marshall G. Johnson, Jr.	JOHNSON MARSHALL G JR

	ACCOUNT #	NAME	INDEXED NAME
113.	2018	Joseph H. Breithaupt	BREITHAUPT JOSEPH H
114.	2033	Dennis M. Quinn	QUINN DENNIS M
115.	2052	Roderick D. Ashley	ASHLEY RODERICK D
116.	2068	Laura L. Worcester	WORCESTER LAURA L
117.	2075	Mohamed Gamal-Eldin	GAMALELDIN MOHAMED
118.	2097	Sarah E. Fields	FIELDS SARAH E
119.	2111	June M. Epstein	EPSTEIN JUNE M
120.	2128	Travis Lee-Dugger	LEEDUGGER TRAVIS
121.	2137	Gabriele C. Piermarini	PIERMARINI GABRIELE C
122.	2152	M. Andrea Hartman	HARTMAN M ANDREA
123.	2167	Kumar S. Goradia	GORADIA KUMAR S
124.	2181	Richard Leeds	LEEDS RICHARD
125.	2195	Neva M. Turano	TURANO NEVA M
126.	2208	Melyni J. Worth	WORTH MELYNI J
127.	2211	Tammy Zysman	ZYSMAN TAMMY
128.	2233	Marco Deleon	DELEON MARCO
129.	2237	Anna K. Vandermeer	VANDERMEER ANNA K
130.	2246	Yolontha S. Chlapowski	CHLAPOWSKI YOLONTHA S
131.	2256	Jan R. Shinol, Jr.	SHINOL JAN R JR
132.	2257	Capt. Ivory Lewis	LEWIS IVORY CAPT
133.	2267	Gregory J. Young	YOUNG GREGORY J
134.	2268	Karen H. Krause-Daniels	KRAUSEDANIELS KAREN H
135.	2270	Christopher J. Dinovi	DINOVI CHRISTOPHER J
136.	2273	Lora-Lee Kelley	KELLEY LORALEE
137.	2275	Damon S. Wright	WRIGHT DAMON S
138.	2282	Barry D. Lawson	LAWSON BARRY D
139.	2290	Marci A. Au	AU MARCI A
140.	2297	Suzette Gamal	GAMAL SUZETTE
141.	2308	David J. Isaacson	ISAACSON DAVID J
142.	2338	Jimmy J. Joyce	JOYCE JIMMY J
143.	2352	Melody Edmonds	EDMONDS MELODY
144.	2370	Stephanie K. Turner	TURNER STEPHANIE K
145.	2391	Denise J. Schuster	SCHUSTER DENISE J
146.	2405	Kelly R. Wright	WRIGHT KELLY R
147.	2416	M. B. Obrien	OBRIEN M B
148.	2444	Kathryn A. Novitski	NOVITSKI KATHRYN A
149.	2458	Anjali Venkateshwaran	VENKATESHWARAN ANJALI
150.	2472	Corazon L. Robera	ROBERA CORAZON L
151.	2491	J. Gallucci-Grow	GALLUCCIGROW J
152.	2508	Teresita M. Ryan	RYAN TERESITA M
153.	2512	Rex M. Blevins	BLEVINS REX M
154.	2528	Chang-Hong Wu	WU CHANGHONG
155.	2542	A. C. Casteneda	CASTENEDA A C
156.	2567	Lisa A. Luxford	LUXFORD LISA A
157.	2601	Don A. Utt	UTT DON A
158.	2612	Stephen P. Howard	HOWARD STEPHEN P
159.	2638	Maryann G. Edmondson	EDMONDSON MARYANN G
160.	2652	Joel C. Skinner	SKINNER JOEL C
161.	2666	David H. Cohen, Jr.	COHEN DAVID H JR
162.	2682	Stephen Turner	TURNER STEPHEN
163.	2697	K. S. Hong, CPA	HONG K S CPA
164.	2703	Jorge Luis Yordan-Hernandez	YORDANHERNANDEZ JORGE LUIS
165.	2731	Roberto P. Gregorio	GREGORIO ROBERTO P
166.	2747	Eric J. Wuchina	WUCHINA ERIC J
167.	2752	Bubba Neal	NEAL BUBBA
168.	2753	Johanne J. Fontaine	FONTAINE JOHANNE J

	ACCOUNT #	NAME	INDEXED NAME
169.	2760	Constance C. Ausbrooks	AUSBROOKS CONSTANCE C
170.	2782	W. Diane Ivey	IVEY W DIANE
171.	2795	Melissa J. Edmonds	EDMONDS MELISSA J
172.	2805	Chang W. Jung	JUNG CHANG W
173.	2830	Ginger M. DuValle	DUVALLE GINGER M
174.	2845	LaBradford Smith	SMITH LABRADFORD
175.	2873	Ulrich Paar	PAAR ULRICH
176.	2894	Stephanie J. Villa	VILLA STEPHANIE J
177.	2911	Paige J. Wynne	WYNNE PAIGE J
178.	2968	Samuel L. Fong	FONG SAMUEL L
179.	2972	Melissa Huston	HUSTON MELISSA
180.	2975	Tracy L. Bohen	BOHEN TRACY L
181.	2981	Patricia R. Reyna	REYNA PATRICIA R
182.	2993	Anne-Marie Grow	GROW ANNEMARIE
183.	3005	Gary W. Tye	TYE GARY W
184.	3009	Margaret Roth	ROTH MARGARET
185.	3012	Paige J. Wynne, Jr.	WYNNE PAIGE J JR
186.	3013	Adela Carmen Castenada	CASTENADA ADELA CARMEN
187.	3016	Rosanna M. Ayres	AYRES ROSANNA M
188.	3023	Sirandasu Soujanyam	SOUJANYAM SIRANDASU
189.	3025	John D. Consoletti	CONSOLETTI JOHN D
190.	3029	Rosa Belle Lemonte	LEMONTE ROSA BELLE
191.	3030	Vicky W. Justice	JUSTICE VICKY W
192.	3032	Dr. Elbert T. Roberts	ROBERTS ELBERT T DR
193.	3034	Nancy E. Parks	PARKS NANCY E
194.	3035	Loraine E. Kelley	KELLEY LORAINE E
195.	3037	Carma J. Stephens	STEPHENS CARMA J
196.	3038	Gregory T. Cooper	COOPER GREGORY T
197.	3039	Elizabeth D. Guynn	GUYNN ELIZABETH D
198.	3040	Theresa D. Pryzby, MD	PRYZBY THERESA D MD
199.	3041	Louis Heath-Camp	HEATHCAMP LOUIS
200.	3042	Kelly R. Von Dohlen	VONDOHLEN KELLY R
201.	3043	Sean O'Hara	OHARA SEAN
202.	3044	Marie H. Rojas	ROJAS MARIE H
203.	3045	Dr. Tony V. Estrella	ESTRELLA TONY V DR
204.	3046	Beth-Anne G. Harper	HARPER BETHANNE G
205.	3047	Stephen L. Wallenstein	WALLENSTEIN STEPHEN L

	ADDRESS	CITY	STATE	ZIP	PHONE
1.	212 Elm Street	Spanish Lake	MO	63137-0435	314-555-7639
2.	1508 American Drive	Alton	IL	62002-0917	618-555-9121
3.	PO Box 387	Spanish Lake	MO	63137-0387	314-555-6478
4.	105 Marina Circle	St. Louis	MO	63114-6328	314-555-2284
5.	104 Grove Road	Spanish Lake	MO	63137-0978	314-555-4378
6.	341 Meadowdale Blvd.	Spanish Lake	MO	63137-1466	314-555-4278
7.	1912 Dresden Road	Florissant	MO	63031-2633	314-555-1045
8.	23 Alexander Avenue	Spanish Lake	MO	63137-1374	314-555-8639
9.	316 Cedar Creek Lane	Granite City	IL	62040-1466	618-555-1430
10.	3801 Plymouth Drive	St. Louis	MO	63111-4622	314-555-1748
11.	PO Box 678	Alton	IL	62002-0678	618-555-8602
12.	126 Willow Oaks Drive	Spanish Lake	MO	63137-1743	314-555-2491
13.	316 Happy Hill Road	Edwardsville	IL	62025-1779	618-555-4428
14.	PO Box 19	Florissant	MO	63032-0019	314-555-1840
15.	510 Trace Court	Spanish Lake	MO	63137-1979	314-555-3637
16.	102 Taylor Avenue	Alton	IL	62002-2375	618-555-8747
17.	703 Baldwin Road	Spanish Lake	MO	63137-1396	314-555-4265
18.	17 Grenada Road	Granite City	IL	62040-1636	618-555-1622
19.	68 East Highbury Drive	Spanish Lake	MO	63137-0884	314-555-7223
20.	152 LaVata Drive	St. Louis	MO	63109-3763	314-555-9704
21.	324 Dunwoody Road	Spanish Lake	MO	63137-2122	314-555-1455
22.	515 Baldwin Road	Spanish Lake	MO	63137-1343	314-555-6285
23.	Route 1, Box 381	Granite City	IL	62040-1556	618-555-6016
24.	PO Box 327	Florissant	MO	63033-0327	314-555-1629
25.	111 Guilford Road	Jennings	MO	63136-0737	314-555-8868
26.	504 Bramblewood	Edwardsville	IL	62025-1893	618-555-3254
27.	Route 2, Box 192	Spanish Lake	MO	63137-0625	314-555-9976
28.	3324 Day Road, Apt. 177	St. Louis	MO	63106-6730	314-555-8894
29.	16 Westbrook Avenue	Spanish Lake	MO	63137-0442	314-555-6070
30.	PO Box 77	Jennings	MO	63136-0077	314-555-6221
31.	526 Lost Forest Drive	Ferguson	MO	63135-1368	314-555-8594
32.	186 Ivanhoe Drive	Alton	IL	62002-1739	618-555-6348
33.	390 Elberton Court	Spanish Lake	MO	63137-0839	314-555-6472
34.	187 Fernbrook Drive	Florissant	MO	63032-1468	314-555-1290
35.	200 Patterson Avenue	Spanish Lake	MO	63137-0912	314-555-7357
36.	4703 West Cornwall	St. Louis	MO	63103-3625	314-555-7633
37.	407 Eastover Avenue	Granite City	IL	62040-1299	618-555-8692
38.	604 Hillside Road	Jennings	MO	63136-1008	314-555-6452
39.	211 Main Street	Spanish Lake	MO	63137-0819	314-555-9932
40.	Route 1, Box 42	Granite City	IL	62040-2144	618-555-1254
41.	331 Lee Park Road	Spanish Lake	MO	63137-0911	314-555-6373
42.	3000 Cherokee Turnpike	Alton	IL	62002-1296	618-555-9908
43.	121 Downy Lane	Spanish Lake	MO	63137-1554	314-555-1795
44.	2003 Windbluff Court	St. Charles	MO	63301-1228	314-555-5665
45.	PO Box 1121	Jennings	MO	63136-1121	314-555-8373
46.	20524 Floyd Avenue	St. Louis	MO	63112-4343	314-555-9097
47.	363 Devonshire Road	Spanish Lake	MO	63137-1003	314-555-2146
48.	314 Oak Glen	Ferguson	MO	63135-2139	314-555-8446
49.	613 South Nansemond	Edwardsville	IL	62025-1265	618-555-3488
50.	149 Repp Circle	Spanish Lake	MO	63137-0436	314-555-2316
51.	455 Rodney Road	Spanish Lake	MO	63137-0112	314-555-7665
52.	3918 Lamplighter Drive	St. Louis	MO	63110-2177	314-555-8436
53.	24 South Dumbarton	Alton	IL	62002-3244	618-555-9076
54.	206 Duncan Street	Ferguson	MO	63135-1668	314-555-5325
55.	Route 4, Box 411	Jennings	MO	63136-1550	314-555-6794
56.	402 Riverside Drive	Edwardsville	IL	62025-2887	618-555-3251

	ADDRESS	CITY	STATE	ZIP	PHONE
57.	31 Seminary Avenue	Jennings	MO	63136-3221	314-555-2749
58.	10401 Hollyberry Drive	St. Louis	MO	63113-4336	314-555-4275
59.	480 Red Oak Lane	Spanish Lake	MO	63137-0995	314-555-9472
60.	808 Weldon Drive	Spanish Lake	MO	63137-1447	314-555-8590
61.	PO Box 434	Florissant	MO	63031-0434	314-555-5007
62.	PO Box 193	Spanish Lake	MO	63137-0193	314-555-3729
63.	5231 Walmsley Avenue	St. Louis	MO	63110-3270	314-555-4358
64.	62 Oakmont Drive	Ferguson	MO	63135-2156	314-555-9459
65.	3121 Hey Road	St. Charles	MO	63301-3721	314-555-1417
66.	318 Foxglove Road	Spanish Lake	MO	63137-1919	314-555-9352
67.	800 Arkwright Circle	Spanish Lake	MO	63137-1239	314-555-8793
68.	11323 North Pocono	St. Louis	MO	63115-2916	314-555-7344
69.	803 Marilea Road	Spanish Lake	MO	63137-0453	314-555-1447
70.	PO Box 419	Spanish Lake	MO	63137-0419	314-555-7499
71.	11125 Saybrook Road	St. Louis	MO	63103-4287	314-555-4426
72.	PO Box 919	Spanish Lake	MO	63137-0919	314-555-6605
73.	Route 3, Box 278	Ferguson	MO	63135-2140	314-555-1584
74.	714 Spottswood Road	Florissant	MO	63032-1271	314-555-3007
75.	710 Fernwood Street	Spanish Lake	MO	63137-0212	314-555-4446
76.	29 Old Hanover Avenue	Spanish Lake	MO	63137-1832	314-555-2794
77.	10706 Solaris Circle	St. Louis	MO	63107-2745	314-555-3648
78.	420 North Allen Avenue	Spanish Lake	MO	63137-1723	314-555-9567
79.	302 Tanners Way	Jennings	MO	63136-2312	314-555-7335
80.	PO Box 909	Spanish Lake	MO	63137-0909	314-555-8869
81.	160 Heritage Drive	Granite City	IL	62040-2581	618-555-2144
82.	PO Box 600	Spanish Lake	MO	63137-0600	314-555-6553
83.	Route 1, Box 14	Spanish Lake	MO	63137-1945	314-555-1434
84.	7010 Bunche Street	St. Louis	MO	63109-1265	314-555-4584
85.	707 East Main Street	Spanish Lake	MO	63137-0666	314-555-6439
86.	930 Lester Lane	Spanish Lake	MO	63137-1921	314-555-4365
87.	8 West Sedgwick Street	Jennings	MO	63136-2891	314-555-6458
88.	Route 5, Box 274	Florissant	MO	63033-4012	314-555-3353
89.	672 Kayhoe Road	Spanish Lake	MO	63137-0217	314-555-7568
90.	PO Box 40432	St. Louis	MO	63114-0432	314-555-9565
91.	16117 Edgewood Drive	St. Louis	MO	63108-3242	314-555-7990
92.	761 Carlton Road	Spanish Lake	MO	63137-1211	314-555-2332
93.	130 Sixth Street	Ferguson	MO	63135-1154	314-555-3754
94.	811 North Yale Avenue	Spanish Lake	MO	63137-0623	314-555-7450
95.	101 Santa Maria Drive	Spanish Lake	MO	63137-1528	314-555-9702
96.	427 23rd Street	St. Louis	MO	63106-3120	314-555-4592
97.	100 South Boulevard	Spanish Lake	MO	63137-0333	314-555-8894
98.	301 Greenway Lane	Florissant	MO	63032-2471	314-555-3468
99.	Greenleigh Mobile Park	Jennings	MO	63136-2172	314-555-2258
100.	Route 5, Box 177	Spanish Lake	MO	63137-0821	314-555-3628
101.	PO Box 1848	Spanish Lake	MO	63137-1848	314-555-9588
102.	3690 Montrose Avenue	St. Louis	MO	63112-2326	314-555-2164
103.	870 Stafford Street	Spanish Lake	MO	63137-1443	314-555-5739
104.	292 Twain Lane	Granite City	IL	62040-2399	618-555-8853
105.	12 Rock Road	Jennings	MO	63136-1777	314-555-5279
106.	1221 Severn Road	Alton	IL	62002-3116	618-555-4244
107.	689 Locust Street	Spanish Lake	MO	63137-0121	314-555-7359
108.	520 Greenford Drive	Spanish Lake	MO	63137-1384	314-555-8806
109.	7526 Landsworth Avenue	St. Louis	MO	63104-3009	314-555-5752
110.	Route 2, Box 552	Spanish Lake	MO	63137-0598	314-555-8462
111.	220 Parkwood Avenue	Florissant	MO	63033-2785	314-555-4474
112.	1213 Deerfield Lane	Jennings	MO	63136-1609	314-555-9605

	ADDRESS	CITY	STATF	ZIP	PHONE
113.	509 Eanes Lane	Spanish Lake	MO	63137-0891	314-555-8483
114.	830 Barbour Road	Spanish Lake	MO	63137-1231	314-555-2387
115.	PO Box 16114	St. Louis	MO	63109-6114	314-555-7493
116.	560 Indigo Road	Spanish Lake	MO	63137-0763	314-555-6383
117.	260 Pleasant Run Drive	Ferguson	MO	63135-3291	314-555-9620
118.	630 Deerwater Court	Spanish Lake	MO	63137-1923	314-555-9503
119.	310 Falcon Road	Spanish Lake	MO	63137-0825	314-555-2617
120.	501 South Davis Avenue	Spanish Lake	MO	63137-1430	314-555-5842
121.	5200 Wingfield Street	St. Louis	MO	63112-3591	314-555-9034
122.	Route 1, Box 424	Spanish Lake	MO	63137-1326	314-555-6387
123.	533 Hempwood Place	Florissant	MO	63031-2548	314-555-3275
124.	130 Barnard Drive	Spanish Lake	MO	63137-1690	314-555-4693
125.	1539A Honeygrove Drive	St. Charles	MO	63301-3176	314-555-1153
126.	141 Carlstone Place	Spanish Lake	MO	63137-0979	314-555-7383
127.	10113 Cutter Drive	St. Louis	MO	63109-2671	314-555-8706
128.	PO Box 191	Spanish Lake	MO	63137-0191	314-555-3077
129.	719 Kenneth Drive	Spanish Lake	MO	63137-0815	314-555-4528
130.	Route 2, Box 89	Jennings	MO	63136-3121	314-555-9562
131.	220 Whistler Road	Spanish Lake	MO	63137-0967	314-555-7757
132.	PO Box 80	Florissant	MO	63033-0080	314-555-2411
133.	111 Barrister Road	Spanish Lake	MO	63137-1476	314-555-6378
134.	252 Merriewood Road	Ferguson	MO	63135-1970	314-555-4288
135.	308 Floyd Avenue	Granite City	IL	62040-0909	618-555-8687
136.	417 Creekview Road	Spanish Lake	MO	63137-0154	314-555-7795
137.	PO Box 638	Spanish Lake	MO	63137-0638	314-555-1555
138.	305 Second Avenue	Spanish Lake	MO	63137-0782	314-555-8352
139.	4027 Lauderdale Road	St. Louis	MO	63102-2615	314-555-9070
140.	2228 Tremont Court	St. Louis	MO	63111-5131	314-555-5877
141.	803 Starboard Drive	Florissant	MO	63032-2866	314-555-6656
142.	103 Ivystone Drive	Spanish Lake	MO	63137-0726	314-555-9846
143.	10308 Delray Boulevard	St. Louis	MO	63108-4352	314-555-2157
144.	200 Noble Avenue	Spanish Lake	MO	63137-1117	314-555-9767
145.	Route 1, Box 68	Spanish Lake	MO	63137-0805	314-555-3670
146.	6304 Sunset Court	St. Louis	MO	63105-4300	314-555-2185
147.	13002 Ashtree Road	St. Louis	MO	63115-1666	314-555-5525
148.	50 Jefferson Drive	Spanish Lake	MO	63137-0325	314-555-7748
149.	608 Prairie Road	Jennings	MO	63136-0286	314-555-3259
150.	214 Warwick Road	Spanish Lake	MO	63137-0196	314-555-5335
151.	419 Blair Street	Edwardsville	IL	62025-1213	618-555-7410
152.	628 Barnett Avenue	Jennings	MO	63136-0556	314-555-6259
153.	506 Smithey Court	Spanish Lake	MO	63137-1487	314-555-3411
154.	702 Beechdale Road	Ferguson	MO	63135-2111	314-555-7395
155.	108 Argyle Terrace	Spanish Lake	MO	63137-0743	314-555-6307
156.	150 Third Street	Spanish Lake	MO	63137-0675	314-555-6338
157.	801 Fitzhugh Avenue	Florissant	MO	63031-1546	314-555-8260
158.	9557 Winston Street	St. Louis	MO	63102-3122	314-555-5138
159.	PO Box 168	Spanish Lake	MO	63137-0168	314-555-5362
160.	303 Woodhurst Drive	Spanish Lake	MO	63137-1201	314-555-9469
161.	8319 Tower Road	St. Charles	MO	63301-1787	314-555-7066
162.	230 Braddock Road	Spanish Lake	MO	63137-0335	314-555-4270
163.	119 Silversmith Court	Spanish Lake	MO	63137-1369	314-555-3144
164.	507 Split Oak Lane	Spanish Lake	MO	63137-0748	314-555-3363
165.	21218 Lexington Drive	St. Louis	MO	63107-3185	314-555-5557
166.	403 Winding Way Road	Granite City	IL	62040-1875	618-555-5280
167.	117 Hollins Place	Jennings	MO	63136-2658	314-555-3697
168.	Route 4, Box 71	Spanish Lake	MO	63137-1006	314-555-1140

	ADDRESS	CITY	STATE	ZIP	PHONE
169.	405 Grace Street	Florissant	MO	63033-3010	314-555-8394
170.	PO Box 618	Spanish Lake	MO	63137-0618	314-555-5590
171.	209 Pennsbury Avenue	Spanish Lake	MO	63137-1288	314-555-4285
172.	6834 Farmington Drive	St. Louis	MO	63112-2091	314-555-6907
173.	927 Franklin Street	Ferguson	MO	63135-0277	314-555-3159
174.	300 Lookout Point	Jennings	MO	63136-2981	314-555-2668
175.	636 Grove Avenue	Spanish Lake	MO	63137-1093	314-555-4006
176.	418 Vandover Road	Spanish Lake	MO	63137-0582	314-555-3445
177.	16300 East Main Street	St. Louis	MO	63114-3528	314-555-8574
178.	231 Spaulding Drive	Alton	IL	62002-3343	618-555-6678
179.	614 Lipton Road	Spanish Lake	MO	63137-1284	314-555-3526
180.	706 Willis Avenue	Spanish Lake	MO	63137-0893	314-555-8583
181.	PO Box 712	Spanish Lake	MO	63137-0712	314-555-6484
182.	217 Futura Avenue	Edwardsville	IL	62025-2167	618-555-6335
183.	Route 3, Box 118	Spanish Lake	MO	63137-0648	314-555-2143
184.	707 Merry, Apt. 416	St. Louis	MO	63109-1991	314-555-5577
185.	104 Santa Rosa	Florissant	MO	63032-2009	314-555-8442
186.	PO Box 72	Spanish Lake	MO	63137-0072	314-555-8539
187.	312 Martha Lane	Spanish Lake	MO	63137-1073	314-555-7956
188.	142 South Oak Avenue	Ferguson	MO	63135-0668	314-555-6884
189.	Route 2, Box 148	Spanish Lake	MO	63137-0826	314-555-3554
190.	233 Hunt Avenue	Spanish Lake	MO	63137-1103	314-555-8978
191.	126 Oakwood Lane	Jennings	MO	63136-2843	314-555-6008
192.	213 Maplewood Avenue	Spanish Lake	MO	63137-1038	314-555-4382
193.	1736 Kenmore Road	St. Charles	MO	63301-3242	314-555-8553
194.	PO Box 163	Spanish Lake	MO	63137-0163	314-555-2389
195.	187 North High Street	Spanish Lake	MO	63137-1987	314-555-9991
196.	801 Ingalls Street	Granite City	IL	62040-1434	618-555-6238
197.	214 Fairfax Street	Ferguson	MO	63135-2413	314-555-7226
198.	375 Clearview Drive	Spanish Lake	MO	63137-1255	314-555-8838
199.	PO Box 133	St. Charles	MO	63301-0133	314-555-8292
200.	965 Cardinal Drive	Spanish Lake	MO	63137-1348	314-555-7810
201.	2803 Chelsea Court	Alton	IL	62002-3291	618-555-9190
202.	104 South Fifth Street	Spanish Lake	MO	63137-2558	314-555-8702
203.	401 Giles Road	Jennings	MO	63136-0825	314-555-3171
204.	Route 2, Box 156	Spanish Lake	MO	63137-0989	314-555-0830
205.	1009 Ascot Lane	St. Louis	MO	63106-5410	314-555-8275

	CREDIT LIMIT	CREDIT RATING		CREDIT LIMIT	CREDIT RATING
1.	500	B	57.	750	C
2.	1000	B	58.	1500	B
3.	1250	B	59.	2000	A
4.	2000	A	60.	500	B
5.	1000	B	61.	500	C
6.	1000	B	62.	1500	B
7.	1250	B	63.	1500	B
8.	1500	B	64.	1000	B
9.	500	B	65.	1500	B
10.	1000	B	66.	1000	B
11.	750	B	67.	750	C
12.	1000	B	68.	1500	B
13.	1500	B	69.	1500	B
14.	2000	A	70.	1500	B
15.	1000	B	71.	2000	A
16.	1750	A	72.	1750	A
17.	1750	A	73.	1000	B
18.	1000	B	74.	1500	B
19.	1000	C	75.	750	C
20.	1000	B	76.	1250	B
21.	500	B	77.	500	B
22.	1500	B	78.	1500	B
23.	1000	B	79.	1000	B
24.	1250	B	80.	1000	C
25.	2000	A	81.	2000	A
26.	1500	B	82.	1000	B
27.	1000	B	83.	1500	B
28.	1750	A	84.	1000	B
29.	750	C	85.	1500	B
30.	1000	B	86.	1000	B
31.	1500	B	87.	1000	B
32.	1500	B	88.	750	C
33.	500	B	89.	500	B
34.	1000	B	90.	1500	B
35.	1000	C	91.	1000	B
36.	1500	B	92.	1500	B
37.	2000	A	93.	1500	B
38.	1000	B	94.	2000	A
39.	750	B	95.	1000	B
40.	1250	B	96.	1500	B
41.	1500	B	97.	500	C
42.	500	C	98.	750	B
43.	1000	B	99.	1500	B
44.	1000	B	100.	1500	B
45.	1000	B	101.	1000	B
46.	1000	B	102.	1250	B
47.	1500	B	103.	1000	B
48.	1500	B	104.	1500	B
49.	1000	C	105.	1000	C
50.	2000	A	106.	500	B
51.	1500	B	107.	1500	B
52.	1750	A	108.	1000	B
53.	1000	B	109.	2000	A
54.	500	B	110.	1500	B
55.	1500	B	111.	1750	A
56.	1000	B	112.	1000	B

	CREDIT LIMIT	CREDIT RATING
113.	2000	A
114.	1000	C
115.	1500	B
116.	500	B
117.	500	B
118.	1500	B
119.	2000	A
120.	1000	B
121.	1250	B
122.	1500	B
123.	2000	B
124.	1000	C
125.	500	B
126.	1000	B
127.	1500	B
128.	2000	A
129.	1000	B
130.	1750	A
131.	1000	B
132.	500	C
133.	1000	B
134.	1500	B
135.	1250	B
136.	750	B
137.	2000	A
138.	1000	C
139.	1500	B
140.	1000	C
141.	1000	B
142.	2000	A
143.	1000	B
144.	1000	B
145.	1500	B
146.	1000	B
147.	1000	C
148.	1500	B
149.	1750	A
150.	1750	A
151.	1000	B
152.	750	B
153.	1500	B
154.	1000	B
155.	1500	B
156.	2000	A
157.	1000	B
158.	500	C
159.	1000	B
160.	1500	B
161.	1000	C
162.	1500	B
163.	1250	B
164.	1000	B
165.	2000	A
166.	1750	B
167.	500	B
168.	1000	B

	CREDIT LIMIT	CREDIT RATING
169.	1500	B
170.	1000	B
171.	750	B
172.	1000	B
173.	2000	A
174.	1000	C
175.	1250	B
176.	500	C
177.	1000	B
178.	1000	B
179.	1500	B
180.	750	C
181.	1000	B
182.	1500	B
183.	2000	A
184.	1000	B
185.	500	C
186.	1000	C
187.	1750	A
188.	1000	B
189.	1500	B
190.	1000	B
191.	750	C
192.	1000	A
193.	1500	B
194.	1000	B
195.	2000	A
196.	500	C
197.	1000	B
198.	1500	A
199.	750	B
200.	1000	B
201.	750	C
202.	750	B
203.	1500	B
204.	1250	B
205.	500	C

NAME ____________

DATE ____________

SCORE ____________

PROJECT FOUR

FIDELITY UNDERWRITERS, INC.

You will recall working with the records of Fidelity Underwriters, Inc. in Project 1. The managers of Fidelity have decided to convert their client records to an electronic database. In this project, you will be responsible for managing the database for the 100 clients of Fidelity.

ASSIGNMENT 22 EXPLORE THE CLIENT FILE

Follow your instructor's directions to load the program and data disks. Retrieve the data disk file named PROJECT4, which is the client file for Fidelity Underwriters, Inc. Explore the file and answer the following questions.

1. What are the names of the fields? (The first answer is given as an example in Lotus; for dBase and Access it would be CLIENT___NO.)

Field Names	Field Names
CLIENT #	State
Region	ZIP
Organization	Phone
Indexed NAME	No. of Employees.
Address	Premiums last year
City	Claims Last year

2a. What is the lowest client number? **2a.** 19

2b. What is the highest client number? **2b.** 866

3. Each client is assigned to one of six regions in the United States. The codes for each region are shown below.

Region Name	Region Code
Northeast	NE
Southeast	SE
North Central	NC
South Central	SC
Northwest	NW
Southwest	SW

What is the region code for client number 312? **3.** SW

4a. Each client's name is entered in the Organization Name field in address, or standard, order and again in the Indexed Name field in indexed order. You will recall that *indexed order* means that the name is written in all capital letters without punctuation. For business and organization names, indexed order also means that if the word *The* appears at the beginning of a name, it is moved to the end of the name in the Indexed Name field. Also, at Fidelity Underwriters, if a client name begins with a number, computer employees are instructed to insert enough zeros in front of the number in the Indexed Name field to have a total of four digits. This enables the operator to sort all clients into correct order according to standard filing rules if an alphabetic listing is needed. What is the indexed name of client number 387? GREATEST YOGURT ON EARTH INC THE

4b. What is the indexed name of client number 285? 0004 BY 4 Vehicle Exchange

4c. What is the indexed name of client number 491? 0400 Brands Candy Company.

5. What is shown in the Address field for client number 433? **5.** Route 5, Box 200

6. Two-letter state abbreviations are used in this file. If you are not familiar with these abbreviations, consult a ZIP code directory. What is the full name of the state in which client number 792 is located? **6.** KS Kansas

7a. The last four digits of the ZIP code, you will recall, form the ZIP extension. If a client has a post office box, the ZIP extension is the last four digits of the post office box number. What is the post office box number of client number 265? **7a.** Box 21200

7b. What is the ZIP extension of this client? **7b.** 1200

8. Telephone companies in the United States reserve the number 555 as the three digits after the area code for use in textbooks and other publications. Note that all phone numbers in the client file include these digits. What is the phone number for client number 828?

8. 213-555-6859

9. How many employees work for client number 438?

9. 4684

10a. *Premiums* are amounts of money received for providing insurance coverage to clients. What is the amount that was received last year from client number 866?

10a. 1 499 575

10b. *Claims* are amounts of money paid to clients for losses and expenses that are covered by insurance. What is the amount that was paid last year to client number 866?

10b. 1 184 664

10c. Did Fidelity receive more than it paid out to this client?

10c. Received more 314 911

NAME ____________

DATE ____________

SCORE ____________

PROJECT FOUR

FIDELITY UNDERWRITERS, INC.

ASSIGNMENT 23 MAKE CHANGES IN THE CLIENT FILE

Following is information needed to make changes in ten client records. After you have made each change, document it by writing the name (or changed name) of the client for whom the change was made. The first item is an example for a change that has already been made.

Client #	Change	Name
0. 407	Number of employees to 946	**0.** Silesia Pet Foods
1. 399	Address to 3600 Industrial Circle and ZIP code extension to 3317	**1.** Ralon Music Company
2. 168	Phone number to 912-555-7890	**2.** ANA Exterminators, Inc
3. 512	Premiums last year to $93,150	**3.** American Political Research Corp.
4. 743	Organization and indexed names to International Wholesalers	**4.** Intra International
5. 837	Claims last year to $21,353	**5.** Luego & Kirk, Ltd
6. 699	Number of employees to 289	**6.** DuPont Design Corporation
7. 465	Premiums last year to $2,238,300 and claims last year to $2,015,378	**7.** Scott Fischman Company
8. ^77 can't find	Phone number to 305-555-6640	**8.** Public Data Corporation
9. 372	Address to PO Box 838 and ZIP code extension to 0838	**9.** Stereo Sound Service
10. 194	Number of employees to 227 and premiums last year to $233,400	**10.** Sun Cycles.

NAME ____________
DATE ____________
SCORE ____________

PROJECT FOUR

FIDELITY UNDERWRITERS, INC.

ASSIGNMENT 24 DELETE RECORDS FROM THE CLIENT FILE

Five of the businesses in the client file no longer purchase their group insurance from Fidelity Underwriters. Use the information below to delete their records. Document the fact that the deletions have been made by writing your initials in the Account Closed By column.

100

Number and Name of Account to Be Closed	Account Closed By
1. 678 Baja Coastal Bonding Company	**1.** RA
2. 219 G R Produce Marts	**2.** RA
3. 343 Bill Allen Construction Company	**3.** RA
4. 792 Office Furniture Maintenance Corp.	**4.** RA
5. 548 Eagle Security Agency	**5.** RA

95

NAME ________________

DATE ________________

SCORE ________________

PROJECT FOUR

FIDELITY UNDERWRITERS, INC.

ASSIGNMENT 25 RETRIEVE INFORMATION FROM CLIENT RECORDS

Certain information about your company's clients has been requested by your supervisor. Write your response to each request in the column at the right. An example is given.

Information Requested	Response
0. Name of client number 309	**0.** The Datacomm Center, Inc.
1. Phone number of client number 618	**1.** 312-555-0746
2. Number of employees of Piedmont Investment, Ltd.	**2.** 229
3. Street address of Vari Comp Systems, Inc.	**3.** 3801 Orcutt Road
4. Region of 4 Seasons Heating Company	**4.** SC
5. Client number of Willowood Enterprises	**5.** 277
6. Name and full address of client number 828	**6.** 1st Bank of California 11501 East Pemberton Los Angelas, CA 90054-6591
7. Claims last year of City of Albany, New York	**7.** 3 299 562
8. Client number and region of United Optical, Inc.	**8.** # 410 SE
9. Phone number of The Camera Center	**9.** 916-555-4656
10. Difference between premiums and claims last year for client number 535 124775 − 98572	**10.** 26 203

Bonus Problems

1a. An executive inquires whether any of our clients do foreign language interpreting. Is some form of the word *interpret* in the Indexed Name field of any client?

1a. 1 (yes)

1b. If so, what is the client's name and phone number?

1b. American Society of Interpreters 202-555-8439

2. Fidelity has received a phone call from a client, but the person receiving the call failed to write down the client's name and telephone area code. The number written down is 555-1111. What is the name of the client and the complete phone number?

2. 1-Stop Quik Stores. 602-555-1111

NAME ____________________

DATE ____________________

SCORE ____________________

PROJECT FOUR

FIDELITY UNDERWRITERS, INC.

ASSIGNMENT 26 RETRIEVE INFORMATION FROM THE CLIENT FILE

In addition to looking up information about individual clients as you did in Assignment 25, you also receive requests to look up information about groups or categories of clients. Write your response to each request in the space provided.

1. How many clients are located in the northeast region? 1. 19

2. What are the names of all clients located in the state of New York?

4. Jewish Community Day Care Center
3. International Wholesalers
1. 400 Brands Candy Company
5. Professional Market Analysis Co.
2. City of Albany, New York

3. How many of our clients have more than 1,000 employees? 3. 12

4. What are the names of our clients who paid premiums in excess of $3 million last year?

1. City of Albany, New York
3. Republic Steel Shelving Co
4. Trans-International Airlines
2. International Wholesalers.

5. What are the names of our clients who paid premiums of less than $30,000 last year?

Public Data Corporation

Kiddies Kollege Learning Center

Luego & Kirk, Ltd , Stereo Sound Service

Σ

6. What is the total amount of the premiums paid last year by all of our clients? Sum — 6. 58 882 000

7. What is the total number of clients in the file? COUNT — 7. 95

8. What is the average of the premiums paid last year per client? AVG — 8. 619810.53

9. What is the total of the claims last year for all of our clients? SUM — 9. 46 648 303

10. What is the average of the claims last year per client? AVG — 10. 491 034.77

Bonus Problems

1. What are the names of our clients in the south central region who have between 100 and 300 employees? Metro-Thermocrete, Inc , Sun Cycles, The Safemasters Company, Perpetual Systems Corporation.

2. What are the names of our clients in Los Angeles whose premiums last year were less than $1 million? Intraworld Exchange Corp.

TNT Aerobics

Suburban Airservice, Inc

Fidelity Savings Association , Six tigers Chinese Restaurants

3. What are the names of our clients whose indexed names begin with the letters *J*, *K*, and *L*?

Kiddies Kollege Learning Centre, L.K. Presley Investment company

Luego & Kirk, Ltd , Jewis Community Day Care Centre,

Luego and Kirk Medical Centers.

NAME ______________

DATE ______________

SCORE ______________

PROJECT FOUR

FIDELITY UNDERWRITERS, INC.

ASSIGNMENT 27 PRACTICE INDEXING NAMES

In setting up records for new clients, you must enter the name of the client and other information into the file. You will be given the name of the business or organization to be entered. Then it will be up to you to enter the name in the Indexed Name field. The purpose of this assignment is to give you practice in writing names of businesses and organizations in indexed form for a computer file. If you are not familiar with the rules for indexing names of businesses and organizations, consult Chapter 5 in the textbook *Professional Records Management*.

Before you complete this assignment, scan the Name and Indexed Name fields in the records in your Fidelity Underwriters, Inc. client file (PROJECT4). Note the following about the indexed names:

1. Each name is written in all-capital letters.
2. All punctuation is omitted.
3. *The* at the beginning of a name is moved to the end.
4. Abbreviations are entered as abbreviations; they are not spelled out.
5. A number at the beginning of a name has enough leading zeros to make it a four-digit number. A number such as *1st* is indexed as *0001* (without the *st*).
6. Symbols such as & and # are spelled out (*and; number*).
7. Hyphenated names are written as one word, or unit, without the hyphen.
8. Names of persons are not transposed if they are part of a business name.

Using the above information as a guide, write the indexed form of each of the following names.

Name	Indexed Name
1. Burlington Manufacturing Co.	1. BURLINGTON MANUFACTURING CO
2. O'Hara Storage Company	2. OHARA STORAGE COMPANY
3. The Weinstein Mfg. Corp.	3. WEINSTEIN MFG CORP THE
4. Charles the Electrician	4. CHARLES THE ELECTRICIAN

5. 3M Corporation — 5. 0003M CORPORATION

6. 4th Street Parking Garage — 6. 0004 STREET PARKING GARGE

7. Clay-Wallenbine Tax Service — 7. CLAYWALLENBINE TAX SERVICE

8. Jody & Elaine Contractors — 8. JODY AND ELAINE CONTRACTORS

9. The # 12 Quik Shop — 9. NUMBER 12 QUIK SHOP THE

10. John Brown Dance Studio — 10. JOHN BROWN DANCE STUDIO

NAME ____________________

DATE ____________________

SCORE ____________________

PROJECT FOUR

FIDELITY UNDERWRITERS, INC.

ASSIGNMENT 28 ADD RECORDS TO THE CLIENT FILE

The forms that follow contain information about ten new clients who have contracted with Fidelity for group insurance. Add the ten new clients to the file. As you do so, determine the indexed form of each name that is given. Write the indexed name in the space provided, as shown on the first form. The Premiums Last Year and Claims Last Year fields are left blank because these are new clients.

CLIENT #: 867 REGION: SW ORGANIZATION NAME: County of Pima, Arizona

INDEXED NAME: PIMA COUNTY OF ARIZONA

ADDRESS: 300 West Mojave Drive CITY: Tucson STATE: AZ

ZIP: 85703-4182 PHONE: 602-555-9803 # OF EMPLOYEES: 427

CLIENT #: 868 REGION: SC ORGANIZATION NAME: Hearn-Kirkwood, Inc.

INDEXED NAME: ____________________

ADDRESS: 7420 Alamo Road CITY: San Antonio STATE: TX

ZIP: 78214-2716 PHONE: 512-555-5717 # OF EMPLOYEES: 133

CLIENT #: 869 REGION: NE ORGANIZATION NAME: The Rockville Co.

INDEXED NAME: ____________________

ADDRESS: 2311 Union Boulevard CITY: Elmira STATE: NY

ZIP: 14903-2071 PHONE: 607-555-1686 # OF EMPLOYEES: 1,163

CLIENT #: 870 REGION: SW ORGANIZATION NAME: 7 Seas Restaurants

INDEXED NAME: ____________________

ADDRESS: 1050 Summit Avenue CITY: San Diego STATE: CA

ZIP: 92115-3624 PHONE: 714-555-2318 # OF EMPLOYEES: 162

CLIENT #: 871 REGION: NC ORGANIZATION NAME: O'Brien Mfg. Company

INDEXED NAME: ______________________________

ADDRESS: 9192 Edwards Street CITY: Wausau STATE: WI

ZIP: 54401-1275 PHONE: 715-555-4948 # OF EMPLOYEES: 468

CLIENT #: 872 REGION: NW ORGANIZATION NAME: Wilson & Cannon, Inc.

INDEXED NAME: ______________________________

ADDRESS: PO Box 1350 CITY: Eugene STATE: OR

ZIP: 97405-1350 PHONE: 503-555-3780 # OF EMPLOYEES: 77

CLIENT #: 873 REGION: SW ORGANIZATION NAME: Steve Brett Home Repair

INDEXED NAME: ______________________________

ADDRESS: 2845 McComas Avenue CITY: Pueblo STATE: CO

ZIP: 81005-0827 PHONE: 303-555-0186 # OF EMPLOYEES: 27

CLIENT #: 874 REGION: SE ORGANIZATION NAME: The Pavilion Hotel

INDEXED NAME: ______________________________

ADDRESS: 10 Spanish Moss Drive CITY: Savannah STATE: GA

ZIP: 31404-2493 PHONE: 912-555-6841 # OF EMPLOYEES: 293

CLIENT #: 875 REGION: SW ORGANIZATION NAME: Ashton Kennels

INDEXED NAME: ______________________________

ADDRESS: 212 Carson Avenue CITY: Carson City STATE: NV

ZIP: 89701-0807 PHONE: 702-555-7812 # OF EMPLOYEES: 32

CLIENT #: 876 REGION: NE ORGANIZATION NAME: Manijeh Electronics

INDEXED NAME: ______________________________

ADDRESS: 5270 River Road CITY: Hartford STATE: CT

ZIP: 06109-5115 PHONE: 203-555-4944 # OF EMPLOYEES: 119

105 records.

NAME ______________________

DATE ______________________

SCORE ______________________

PROJECT FOUR

FIDELITY UNDERWRITERS, INC.

ASSIGNMENT 29 PRINT CLIENT INFORMATION

Fidelity Underwriter's client file is often used to print lists, labels, and reports of various types. In this assignment, you will use the file to comply with requests for printed information. After completing each printing job, answer the question related to it in the space provided.

1a. Print a mailing label for each client living in the northwest region who paid more than $100,000 in premiums last year.

Hand in 5162-label ALL CAPS USA/RA

1b. How many labels did you print? **1b.** 8.

2a. Print a list of organization names and numbers of employees of all clients in the south central region. Arrange the list in alphabetic order sorted by indexed name. Do NOT PRINT

2b. How many clients are on the list? **2b.** 14

3a. Print a list of organization names and premiums last year for clients whose premiums were between $1 million and $2 million. Arrange the list in descending order sorted by amount of premium. Do not print

3b. What is the largest premium amount on the list? **3b.** 6

Bonus Problems

1. Prepare a pie chart (circle graph) showing the total premiums last year of each of the six regions of Fidelity Underwriters, Inc.

2. Prepare a bar graph comparing the total premiums and claims last year by region.

DON'T DO.

NAME ____________________

DATE ____________________

SCORE ____________________

PROJECT FOUR

FIDELITY UNDERWRITERS, INC.

ASSIGNMENT 30 PROJECT QUIZ

Before you take this quiz, you should have completed the previous assignments so that your client file will be completely updated. You will use the client file at your computer to answer the questions.

1. How many records are in the client file for Fidelity Underwriters, Inc.?

1. 105

2a. What is the number of employees in the organization whose client number is 868?

2a. 133

2b. Change this number of employees to 142. Document the change by writing the name of the client.

2b. ✓

3a. What is the name of the organization whose client number is 565?

3a. Olympic Sporting Goods

3b. Delete this client record from the file, and document the deletion by writing your initials.

3b. RA

4. Add a record to the client file using the information on the following form. Write the indexed name of the new client in the space provided.

CLIENT #: 877 REGION: NC ORGANIZATION NAME: The Chicago Mfg. Co.

INDEXED NAME: CHICAGO MFG CO THE

ADDRESS: 18202 Stockyard Road CITY: Chicago STATE: IL

ZIP: 60614-3326 PHONE: 312-555-8848 # OF EMPLOYEES: 545

5. What are the premiums last year and claims last year for client number 822? P=867150 C=563648

6. How many employees does Professional Market Analysis Co. have? **6.** 694

7. What are the names of the clients who have fewer than 30 employees?

Luego & Kirk, Ltd, Public Data Corporation, Steve Brett Home Repair.

8. For how many clients in the southwest region were premiums last year greater than $200,000? **8.** 14

9. For all clients who are located in the north central region, what is the total number of employees? **9.** 5934

10. Print an alphabetic list, sorted by indexed name, of the organization names, premiums last year, and claims last year for all clients located in the southwest region. There will be no premium or claim amounts for new clients who have been added to the file. How many names are on the list? Attach the list to this quiz and give it to your instructor. **10.** 28

AVERAGE Premiums = 625 159.3
Claim = 495 225.2
Highest " = 8782500
" = 7289475
TOTAL # OF Employees = 51845

Project Four (Printout of Database After Completion of All Assignments Except Quiz)

	CLIENT #	REGION	ORGANIZATION NAME
1.	19	NC	Interstate Motels
2.	33	NE	Pier 4 Import Agency
3.	51	NW	Mr. Monro Jeans Mfgrs.
4.	77	SE	Public Data Corporation
5.	90	NE	City of Albany, New York
6.	98	SW	California Excavators, Inc.
7.	115	NE	Rockville Steel & Mfg. Co.
8.	119	SC	Kiddies Kollege Learning Center
9.	126	SW	United Refrigeration, Inc.
10.	152	SW	Pier Nine Pacific Seafood
11.	166	SC	Metro-Thermocrete, Inc.
12.	168	SE	ANA Exterminators, Inc.
13.	179	NW	American Combustion, Inc.
14.	194	SC	Sun Cycles
15.	203	NC	Rowley-Scher Reprographics
16.	215	SW	Tri-State K-9 Service
17.	222	SE	Randolph Hills Nursing Homes
18.	224	SE	Young & Janetis Company
19.	239	NW	Royce Distributors, Inc.
20.	259	NC	Computerpro, Ltd.
21.	265	SW	Intraworld Exchange Corp.
22.	277	SW	Willowood Enterprises
23.	280	SW	Monrovia Landscape Services
24.	285	SE	4 by 4 Vehicle Exchange
25.	288	SC	L. K. Presley Investment Company
26.	293	SC	The Safemasters Company
27.	298	NC	Columbus Veterinary Hospital
28.	302	SW	The Camera Center
29.	309	NW	The Datacomm Center, Inc.
30.	312	SW	TNT Aerobics
31.	318	NE	Republic Steel Shelving Co.
32.	322	NE	Professional Market Analysis Co.
33.	340	NE	American Society of Interpreters
34.	348	NW	Southlawn Answering Service
35.	352	NW	County of Albany, Wyoming
36.	372	NC	Stereo Sound Service
37.	383	SW	Suburban Airservice, Inc.
38.	387	SC	The Greatest Yogurt on Earth, Inc.
39.	394	SW	1-Stop Quik Stores
40.	399	NW	Ralon Music Company
41.	405	SW	Gateways Unlimited
42.	407	NC	Silesia Pet Foods
43.	410	SE	United Optical, Inc.
44.	423	NE	Professional Mgmt. Consultants
45.	433	SW	Consolidated Copper Mines, Inc.
46.	438	SW	Trans-International Airlines
47.	449	NC	Wyrick Engineering, Inc.
48.	465	NE	Scott Fischman Company
49.	469	NE	Stonestreet Printing & Graphics
50.	490	SW	Marge Goss of Santa Barbara
51.	491	NE	400 Brands Candy Company
52.	509	NC	Quest Systems, Inc.
53.	512	NE	American Political Research Corp.
54.	514	SW	R. Preston Shaw Models
55.	519	SW	Buttons & Badges, Inc.

	CLIENT #	REGION	ORGANIZATION NAME
56.	523	NW	Rosen's Animal Hospitals
57.	535	NE	National Business Lists, Inc.
58.	538	SE	Watkins Digital Thermometers
59.	543	SC	Penril Data Communications Co.
60.	547	SC	4 Seasons Heating Company
61.	552	NW	Sandana Corporation
62.	557	SE	IKO Real Estate, Inc.
63.	565	SW	Olympic Sporting Goods
64.	577	NE	A #1 Auto Rental
65.	590	SW	Fidelity Savings Association
66.	615	SW	Hendricks Booking Agy., Inc.
67.	618	NC	Unicorn Galleries
68.	627	SC	Audiokrafters
69.	645	SE	Gladiator Sports & Awards
70.	658	SE	ZS Commercial Signs Company
71.	661	NC	Teletechnics Corporation
72.	669	SW	Six Tigers Chinese Restaurants
73.	673	SC	Vari Comp Systems, Inc.
74.	674	NW	Samuel C. Boyd & Son, Inc.
75.	676	NW	The Rose Garden Flower Shops
76.	681	SC	Perpetual Systems Corporation
77.	688	SW	Southern California Excavators
78.	691	NE	Forty-Niners Diamond Brokers
79.	699	NE	DuPont Design Corporation
80.	700	SE	Pier 901 Food Exports
81.	702	NC	Poly Method Driving Schools
82.	709	NE	Yorktowne Business Institute
83.	711	SW	Western Credit, Inc.
84.	739	NE	Munford, Mattingly, & Associates
85.	743	NE	International Wholesalers
86.	767	NW	Pacific Research Corporation
87.	773	NC	Wordpro Personnel Services
88.	791	SE	Piedmont Investment, Ltd.
89.	810	NW	Digital Computer Micrographics
90.	822	SW	M'lady Cosmetics Corporation
91.	828	SW	1st Bank of California
92.	837	SC	Luego & Kirk, Ltd.
93.	838	NE	Jewish Community Day Care Centers
94.	865	SC	Luego and Kirk Medical Centers
95.	866	NC	Fidelity Savings of America
96.	867	SW	County of Pima, Arizona
97.	868	SC	Hearn-Kirkwood, Inc.
98.	869	NE	The Rockville Co.
99.	870	SW	7 Seas Restaurants
100.	871	NC	O'Brien Mfg. Company
101.	872	NW	Wilson & Cannon, Inc.
102.	873	SW	Steve Brett Home Repair
103.	874	SE	The Pavilion Hotel
104.	875	SW	Ashton Kennels
105.	876	NE	Manijeh Electronics

	INDEXED NAME	ADDRESS
1.	INTERSTATE MOTELS	13201 Ramblewood Drive
2.	PIER 4 IMPORT AGENCY	7510 Greengate Drive
3.	MR MONRO JEANS MFGRS	800 Rodeo Circle
4.	PUBLIC DATA CORPORATION	PO Box 10001
5.	ALBANY CITY OF NEW YORK	PO Box 32932
6.	CALIFORNIA EXCAVATORS INC	10 North 14th Street
7.	ROCKVILLE STEEL AND MFG CO	PO Box 3246
8.	KIDDIES KOLLEGE LEARNING CENTER	4914 Belmont Avenue
9.	UNITED REFRIGERATION INC	3243 Cactus Trail
10.	PIER NINE PACIFIC SEAFOOD	30 Harbor Avenue
11.	METROTHERMOCRETE INC	1214 Glenside Drive
12.	ANA EXTERMINATORS INC	PO Box 800
13.	AMERICAN COMBUSTION INC	Ninth and Hanover Streets
14.	SUN CYCLES	PO Box 6400
15.	ROWLEYSCHER REPROGRAPHICS	209 Franklin Road
16.	TRISTATE K9 SERVICE	2900 Las Vegas Boulevard
17.	RANDOLPH HILLS NURSING HOMES	1640 Marshall Street
18.	YOUNG AND JANETIS COMPANY	410 Jefferson Street
19.	ROYCE DISTRIBUTORS INC	222 Carousel Lane
20.	COMPUTERPRO LTD	5118 Bending Branch Drive
21.	INTRAWORLD EXCHANGE CORP	PO Box 21200
22.	WILLOWOOD ENTERPRISES	2000 Trenton Avenue
23.	MONROVIA LANDSCAPE SERVICES	1850 Golden Gate Blvd.
24.	0004 BY 4 VEHICLE EXCHANGE	1415 Opryland Drive
25.	L K PRESLEY INVESTMENT COMPANY	2521 Wildercroft Road
26.	SAFEMASTERS COMPANY THE	PO Box 726
27.	COLUMBUS VETERINARY HOSPITAL	1708 West Delaware Avenue
28.	CAMERA CENTER THE	2000 Capitol Boulevard
29.	DATACOMM CENTER INC THE	PO Box 9027
30.	TNT AEROBICS	PO Box 31429
31.	REPUBLIC STEEL SHELVING CO	4000 Industrial Blvd.
32.	PROFESSIONAL MARKET ANALYSIS CO	3443 Wall Street
33.	AMERICAN SOCIETY OF INTERPRETERS	2703 Connecticut Avenue
34.	SOUTHLAWN ANSWERING SERVICE	PO Box 8532
35.	ALBANY COUNTY OF WYOMING	PO Box 1000
36.	STEREO SOUND SERVICE	PO Box 838
37.	SUBURBAN AIRSERVICE INC	1000 Airport Boulevard
38.	GREATEST YOGURT ON EARTH INC THE	405 West Hilliard Road
39.	0001STOP QUIK STORES	4120 Indian River Drive
40.	RALON MUSIC COMPANY	3600 Industrial Circle
41.	GATEWAYS UNLIMITED	1814 Berkeley Boulevard
42.	SILESIA PET FOODS	5110 Tomlynn Street
43.	UNITED OPTICAL INC	6420 Peachtree Street
44.	PROFESSIONAL MGMT CONSULTANTS	3602 Hull Street
45.	CONSOLIDATED COPPER MINES INC	Route 5, Box 200
46.	TRANSINTERNATIONAL AIRLINES	1200 Airport Boulevard
47.	WYRICK ENGINEERING INC	3001 Fifth Avenue
48.	SCOTT FISCHMAN COMPANY	7406 Elkhart Road
49.	STONESTREET PRINTING AND GRAPHICS	11943 Westwood Street
50.	MARGE GOSS OF SANTA BARBARA	990 Azalea Drive
51.	0400 BRANDS CANDY COMPANY	214 Paxton Road
52.	QUEST SYSTEMS INC	4200 Michigan Avenue
53.	AMERICAN POLITICAL RESEARCH CORP	5000 Grove Avenue
54.	R PRESTON SHAW MODELS	420 North Vine Street
55.	BUTTONS AND BADGES INC	11432 Surrey Road

	INDEXED NAME	ADDRESS
56.	ROSENS ANIMAL HOSPITALS	100 Rigsby Street
57.	NATIONAL BUSINESS LISTS INC	309 Wilkinson Street
58.	WATKINS DIGITAL THERMOMETERS	2000 Bluegrass Drive
59.	PENRIL DATA COMMUNICATIONS CO	5855 Deepwater Road
60.	0004 SEASONS HEATING COMPANY	PO Box 1741
61.	SANDANA CORPORATION	806 Emmett Drive
62.	IKO REAL ESTATE INC	Route 1, Box 277
63.	OLYMPIC SPORTING GOODS	6823 Kensington Avenue
64.	A NUMBER1 AUTO RENTAL	2103 West Main Street
65.	FIDELITY SAVINGS ASSOCIATION	820 Guilford Road
66.	HENDRICKS BOOKING AGY INC	600 Hollywood Boulevard
67.	UNICORN GALLERIES	PO Box 7127
68.	AUDIOKRAFTERS	8405 Roslyn Avenue
69.	GLADIATOR SPORTS AND AWARDS	9538 Spanish Moss Trace
70.	ZS COMMERCIAL SIGNS COMPANY	4800 Berrybrook Drive
71.	TELETECHNICS CORPORATION	PO Box 989
72.	SIX TIGERS CHINESE RESTAURANTS	10711 Chipewyan Drive
73.	VARI COMP SYSTEMS INC	3801 Orcutt Road
74.	SAMUEL C BOYD AND SON INC	2520 Brookwood Road
75.	ROSE GARDEN FLOWER SHOPS THE	Route 1, Box 424
76.	PERPETUAL SYSTEMS CORPORATION	237 Lancaster Avenue
77.	SOUTHERN CALIFORNIA EXCAVATORS	121 Monte Sano
78.	FORTYNINERS DIAMOND BROKERS	PO Box 84
79.	DUPONT DESIGN CORPORATION	3220 Goodwin Road
80.	PIER 901 FOOD EXPORTS	2007 Coastal Highway
81.	POLY METHOD DRIVING SCHOOLS	701 Hull Street
82.	YORKTOWNE BUSINESS INSTITUTE	827 East-West Highway
83.	WESTERN CREDIT INC	10360 Chester Road
84.	MUNFORD MATTINGLY AND ASSOCIATES	Route 2, Box 717
85.	INTERNATIONAL WHOLESALERS	3443 Sixth Avenue
86.	PACIFIC RESEARCH CORPORATION	1504 Santa Rosa Road
87.	WORDPRO PERSONNEL SERVICES	827 New Glarus Drive
88.	PIEDMONT INVESTMENT LTD	3127 Military Road
89.	DIGITAL COMPUTER MICROGRAPHICS	3318 West Thompson Street
90.	MLADY COSMETICS CORPORATION	4000 Rocky Mountain Blvd.
91.	0001 BANK OF CALIFORNIA	11501 East Pemberton
92.	LUEGO AND KIRK LTD	7727 Gulf Coast Highway
93.	JEWISH COMMUNITY DAY CARE CENTERS	PO Box 6343
94.	LUEGO AND KIRK MEDICAL CENTERS	7747 Gulf Coast Highway
95.	FIDELITY SAVINGS OF AMERICA	314A North Second Street
96.	PIMA COUNTY OF ARIZONA	300 West Mojave Drive
97.	HEARNKIRKWOOD INC	7420 Alamo Road
98.	ROCKVILLE CO THE	2311 Union Boulevard
99.	0007 SEAS RESTAURANTS	1050 Summit Avenue
100.	OBRIEN MFG COMPANY	9192 Edwards Street
101.	WILSON AND CANNON INC	PO Box 1350
102.	STEVE BRETT HOME REPAIR	2845 McComas Avenue
103.	PAVILION HOTEL THE	10 Spanish Moss Drive
104.	ASHTON KENNELS	212 Carson Avenue
105.	MANIJEH ELECTRONICS	5270 River Road

	CITY	STATE	ZIP	PHONE	# OF EMPLOYEES
1.	Lincoln	NE	68501-2560	402-555-2393	247
2.	Portland	ME	04101-0632	207-555-1669	170
3.	Casper	WY	82601-2699	307-555-4309	412
4.	Miami	FL	33155-0001	305-555-6640	18
5.	Albany	NY	12212-2932	518-555-9014	2,709
6.	Eureka	CA	95501-0587	707-555-6458	92
7.	Pittsburgh	PA	15218-3246	412-555-7684	517
8.	Fort Worth	TX	76102-2139	817-555-0946	34
9.	Phoenix	AZ	85025-5465	602-555-7175	141
10.	San Diego	CA	92197-5409	619-555-3918	362
11.	Oklahoma City	OK	73124-1942	405-555-1191	196
12.	Macon	GA	31213-0800	912-555-7890	85
13.	Seattle	WA	98110-4119	206-555-3681	1,256
14.	San Antonio	TX	78285-6400	512-555-2974	227
15.	Cedar Rapids	IA	52401-4871	319-555-6648	89
16.	Las Vegas	NV	89115-2917	702-555-1332	37
17.	Fort Myers	FL	33906-0897	813-555-4691	314
18.	Roanoke	VA	24024-0645	703-555-1772	222
19.	Billings	MT	59101-6714	406-555-3097	219
20.	Minneapolis	MN	55402-6420	612-555-3461	640
21.	Los Angeles	CA	90052-1200	213-555-3829	836
22.	Riverside	CA	92507-1064	714-555-2979	438
23.	San Francisco	CA	94185-4976	415-555-1611	108
24.	Nashville	TN	37205-6281	615-555-3313	56
25.	Kansas City	MO	64109-5804	816-555-8987	79
26.	Little Rock	AR	72233-0726	501-555-6482	270
27.	Columbus	OH	43218-0587	614-555-3884	43
28.	Sacramento	CA	95814-0921	916-555-4656	66
29.	Vancouver	WA	98661-9027	206-555-9486	291
30.	Los Angeles	CA	90061-1429	213-555-5837	238
31.	Pittsburgh	PA	15220-3464	412-555-3926	2,473
32.	New York	NY	10009-6487	718-555-4873	694
33.	Washington	DC	20015-5191	202-555-8439	1,874
34.	Boise	ID	83708-8532	208-555-9134	74
35.	Laramie	WY	82070-1000	307-555-6890	61
36.	Bismarck	ND	58501-0838	701-555-2169	44
37.	Los Angeles	CA	90057-6437	213-555-7403	129
38.	Wichita	KS	67276-1338	316-555-0658	372
39.	Tucson	AZ	85727-1031	602-555-1111	474
40.	Spokane	WA	99211-3317	509-555-6006	83
41.	Oakland	CA	94616-2154	415-555-3097	2,490
42.	Detroit	MI	48234-5505	313-555-7764	946
43.	Atlanta	GA	30306-2574	404-555-2160	155
44.	Philadelphia	PA	19107-4682	215-555-6611	243
45.	Ogden	UT	84404-0717	801-555-7665	1,250
46.	Los Angeles	CA	90055-1899	213-555-8060	4,684
47.	Rapid City	SD	57701-1064	605-555-4464	47
48.	Boston	MA	02210-1573	617-555-4930	2,076
49.	Newark	NJ	07101-4519	201-555-3000	184
50.	Santa Barbara	CA	93102-0916	714-555-6642	31
51.	Rochester	NY	14692-2151	716-555-8000	350
52.	Chicago	IL	60613-3406	312-555-9393	492
53.	Baltimore	MD	21235-2587	301-555-6874	166
54.	Hollywood	CA	90028-2805	213-555-3927	107
55.	Phoenix	AZ	85027-6428	602-555-4929	254

	CITY	STATE	ZIP	PHONE	# OF EMPLOYEES
56.	Medford	OR	97501-1670	503-555-3970	452
57.	New Haven	CT	06512-0954	203-555-8090	161
58.	Lexington	KY	40513-1418	606-555-1967	347
59.	Houston	TX	77208-5272	713-555-8483	683
60.	Beaumont	TX	77704-1741	409-555-5479	87
61.	Helena	MT	59601-0416	406-555-6703	276
62.	Montgomery	AL	36120-1240	205-555-6664	132
63.	San Francisco	CA	94190-6548	415-555-5731	151
64.	Wilmington	DE	19850-0436	302-555-5039	73
65.	Los Angeles	CA	90050-4831	213-555-4098	396
66.	Hollywood	CA	90028-3648	213-555-9916	86
67.	Chicago	IL	60609-7127	312-555-0746	173
68.	Oklahoma City	OK	73126-3524	405-555-9798	894
69.	New Orleans	LA	70115-5197	504-555-6373	268
70.	Jackson	MS	39206-2468	601-555-5484	146
71.	Milwaukee	WI	53202-0989	414-555-6428	507
72.	Los Angeles	CA	90048-4729	213-555-9617	181
73.	Dallas	TX	75262-1460	214-555-4609	1,294
74.	Portland	OR	97208-0745	503-555-3332	45
75.	Olympia	WA	98502-0847	206-555-3790	99
76.	Springfield	MO	65801-0333	417-555-3239	274
77.	Laguna Hills	CA	92653-0316	714-555-0206	142
78.	Manchester	NH	03105-0084	603-555-1006	118
79.	Wilmington	DE	19851-0757	302-555-4718	289
80.	Tampa	FL	33630-1141	813-555-1452	189
81.	Indianapolis	IN	46210-2760	317-555-1006	67
82.	Bethesda	MD	20014-0250	301-555-4691	81
83.	Flagstaff	AZ	86001-1687	602-555-3129	213
84.	Burlington	VT	05401-0203	802-555-8858	35
85.	New York	NY	10015-8184	212-555-3669	3,283
86.	Seattle	WA	98112-3226	206-555-2992	209
87.	Madison	WI	53709-2461	608-555-4391	163
88.	Norfolk	VA	23502-1546	804-555-1335	229
89.	Spokane	WA	99210-0554	509-555-4658	447
90.	Denver	CO	80204-4519	303-555-3675	846
91.	Los Angeles	CA	90054-6591	213-555-6859	3,609
92.	Corpus Christi	TX	78410-2154	512-555-8091	27
93.	Syracuse	NY	13221-6343	315-555-6079	158
94.	Corpus Christi	TX	78409-6514	512-555-3491	33
95.	Omaha	NE	68108-1637	402-555-4628	1,463
96.	Tucson	AZ	85703-4182	602-555-9803	427
97.	San Antonio	TX	78214-2716	512-555-5717	133
98.	Elmira	NY	14903-2071	607-555-1686	1,163
99.	San Diego	CA	92115-3624	714-555-2318	162
100.	Wausau	WI	54401-1275	715-555-4948	468
101.	Eugene	OR	97405-1350	503-555-3780	77
102.	Pueblo	CO	81005-0827	303-555-0186	27
103.	Savannah	GA	31404-2493	912-555-6841	293
104.	Carson City	NV	89701-0807	702-555-7812	32
105.	Hartford	CT	06109-5115	203-555-4944	119

	PREMIUMS LAST YEAR	CLAIMS LAST YEAR
1.	135,850	107,322
2.	131,750	109,353
3.	226,600	160,886
4.	25,200	16,380
5.	3,792,600	3,299,562
6.	172,500	136,275
7.	969,375	688,256
8.	26,350	21,871
9.	144,525	102,613
10.	506,800	420,644
11.	367,500	260,925
12.	159,375	103,594
13.	2,355,000	1,860,450
14.	233,400	207,583
15.	68,975	54,490
16.	51,800	45,066
17.	172,700	122,617
18.	122,100	79,365
19.	224,475	177,335
20.	656,000	518,240
21.	459,800	400,026
22.	339,450	268,166
23.	202,500	143,775
24.	57,400	45,346
25.	43,450	34,326
26.	378,000	313,740
27.	80,625	66,919
28.	36,300	25,773
29.	160,050	126,440
30.	333,200	216,580
31.	4,636,875	3,663,131
32.	537,850	424,902
33.	1,030,700	814,253
34.	57,350	47,601
35.	62,525	49,395
36.	24,200	17,182
37.	241,875	191,081
38.	381,300	301,227
39.	663,600	471,156
40.	64,325	53,390
41.	1,929,750	1,678,883
42.	1,324,400	940,324
43.	158,875	131,866
44.	133,650	105,584
45.	2,343,750	2,039,063
46.	8,782,500	7,289,475
47.	65,800	54,614
48.	2,238,300	2,015,378
49.	257,600	203,504
50.	31,775	25,102
51.	490,000	318,500
52.	381,300	270,723
53.	93,150	72,127
54.	109,675	91,030
55.	355,600	252,476

	PREMIUMS LAST YEAR	CLAIMS LAST YEAR
56.	632,800	499,912
57.	124,775	98,572
58.	190,850	135,504
59.	529,325	418,167
60.	163,125	128,869
61.	282,900	223,491
62.	135,300	96,063
63.	117,025	97,131
64.	102,200	72,562
65.	217,800	172,062
66.	120,400	95,116
67.	177,325	115,261
68.	1,676,250	1,089,563
69.	207,700	180,699
70.	273,750	216,263
71.	392,925	278,977
72.	185,525	153,986
73.	1,811,600	1,431,164
74.	63,000	44,730
75.	76,725	60,613
76.	212,350	167,757
77.	198,800	165,004
78.	120,950	78,618
79.	279,825	198,676
80.	264,600	219,618
81.	125,625	99,244
82.	62,775	49,592
83.	165,075	143,615
84.	35,875	31,211
85.	4,596,200	3,630,998
86.	214,225	177,807
87.	167,075	131,989
88.	234,725	185,433
89.	346,425	225,176
90.	867,150	563,648
91.	2,796,975	1,985,852
92.	27,675	21,353
93.	122,450	96,736
94.	33,825	26,722
95.	1,499,575	1,184,664
96.		
97.		
98.		
99.		
100.		
101.		
102.		
103.		
104.		
105.		

NAME ____________________

DATE ____________________

SCORE ____________________

PROJECT FIVE

NEW AGE OFFICE SUPPLY

You will recall working with the records of New Age Office Supply in Project 1. The managers of New Age have decided to convert their client records to an electronic database. In this project, you will be responsible for managing the database for the 200 products in the New Age Office Supply inventory.

ASSIGNMENT 31 EXPLORE THE INVENTORY FILE

Follow your instructor's direction to load the program and data disks. Retrieve the data disk file named PROJECT5, which is the inventory file for New Age Office Supply. Explore the file and answer the following questions.

1. What are the names of the fields? (The first answer is given as an example in Lotus; for dBase and Access it would be Product___CO.)

Field Names	Field Names	
PRODUCT CODE	Unit-cost	Inventory
Descriptio	Selling-pr	
Supplier	on-hand	

2. Each product code begins with a letter of the alphabet, *A* through *H*, which refers to the product class, such as furniture. The letter is followed by a single digit, a hyphen, and four additional digits. Because each product has a distinctive product code, the Product Code field is the key field for this file. How many product codes begin with the letter *F*?

2. 23

3. The Description field contains a brief description of each product. Because descriptions are usually unique, this field can also be used as a key field in this type of file. What is the description of product code E3-0258? ~~Slim Underarm Portfolio~~ Disk pack carrying case

4. The Supplier field names the company from which each product is purchased by New Age Office Supply. Note that the names of most suppliers appear several times in the Supplier field. What is the name of the supplier of product code H1-0314? Quality Office Systems.

5. The Unit Cost field shows the amount paid by New Age Office Supply for each product. These amounts change periodically, of course, as suppliers raise and lower their prices. What is our cost for product code B1-0216? **5.** 98.02.

6. The amount charged by New Age Office Supply for each product has been entered in the Selling Price field. This amount is based on several factors, including unit cost and sales volume. Thus the amounts in this field are also updated periodically. What is the selling price of the product for which you found the cost in Question 5, above? **6.** 169.00

7. The difference between unit cost and selling price is called *gross margin*. This amount is the profit made on a product before the expenses of doing business are deducted. Figure the gross margin for product code B1-0216, and list it in the blank. (See Questions 5 and 6, above.) **7.** 70.98

8. The number of items in stock for each product is entered in the On Hand field. This number is decreased when sales are recorded and increased when products are received from suppliers. How many items of product code A3-0256 are on hand? **8.** 140

9. Each amount in the Inventory Cost field is the total amount paid by New Age Office Supply for the current inventory of a product. Inventory cost has been calculated by multiplying the unit cost of each item by the number of items on hand. What is the inventory cost for product code D1-0284? **9.** 1114.26

10a. What are the unit cost and number on hand for product code G1-0277? **10a.** 161.37 11

10b. Has the inventory cost been calculated and recorded in the inventory file correctly for this product code? **10b.** yes.

NAME ______________

DATE ______________

SCORE ______________

PROJECT FIVE

NEW AGE OFFICE SUPPLY

ASSIGNMENT 32 RECORD SALES IN THE INVENTORY FILE

omit

As products are sold by New Age Office Supply, the number on hand in the computer file must be decreased to show the new number on hand. One of your jobs is to update the inventory file to reflect daily sales. In this assignment, you will be given the product code and the number of items sold. Use this information to calculate the updated number on hand and the updated inventory cost for each product. Follow these steps: (1) subtract the number sold from the number on hand to find the updated number on hand; (2) multiply the updated number on hand by the unit cost of the product to find the updated inventory cost. (Your database software may be capable of doing these computations for you.) Enter the updated amounts in your inventory file in the On Hand field and the Inventory Cost field. Document the entries by writing the updated amounts in the spaces provided below. The first item is an example for a product that has already been updated in the computer file.

Product Code	# Sold	Updated # on Hand	Updated Inventory Cost
0. A1-0252	1	2	$30.24
1. A2-0299	3	______	______
2. A3-0344	1	______	______
3. A4-0113	2	______	______
4. B1-0156	4	______	______
5. B1-0206	2	______	______
6. B2-0184	3	______	______
7. B4-0154	50	______	______
8. C1-0317	9	______	______
9. C2-0388	4	______	______

Product Code	# Sold	Updated # on Hand	Updated Inventory Cost
10. D1-0168	3	________	________________
11. D1-0425	12	________	________________
12. D2-0232	1	________	________________
13. E1-0168	9	________	________________
14. E2-0258	5	________	________________
15. E2-0478	2	________	________________
16. F1-0278	23	________	________________
17. F2-0163	1	________	________________
18. F2-0254	3	________	________________
19. G1-0138	1	________	________________
20. G3-0268	32	________	________________
21. G4-0224	2	________	________________
22. H1-0135	19	________	________________
23. H1-0254	6	________	________________
24. H1-0429	25	________	________________
25. H2-0245	2	________	________________

NAME ____________

DATE ____________

SCORE ____________

PROJECT FIVE

NEW AGE OFFICE SUPPLY

ASSIGNMENT 33 RECORD RECEIPTS IN THE INVENTORY FILE

omit

In Assignment 32, you *decreased* the inventory levels and values as a result of sales. In this assignment, you will *increase* inventory levels and values as a result of receiving products from suppliers. As products are received by New Age Office Supply, the number on hand in the computer file must be increased to show the new number on hand. It is your job to update the inventory file to reflect these receipts. In this assignment, you will be given the product code and the number of items received. Use this information to calculate the updated number on hand and the updated inventory cost for each product. Follow these steps: (1) add the number received to the number on hand to find the updated number on hand; (2) multiply the updated number on hand by the unit cost of the product to find the updated inventory cost. (Your database software may be capable of doing these computations for you.) Enter the updated amounts in your inventory file in the On Hand field and the Inventory Cost field. Document the entries by writing the updated amounts in the spaces provided below. The first item is an example for a product that has already been updated in the computer file.

Product Code	# Received	Updated # on Hand	Updated Inventory Cost
0. A2-0267	1	2	$798.66
1. A3-0421	6	______	______
2. B2-0135	3	______	______
3. C2-0349	36	______	______
4. D1-0323	18	______	______
5. D1-0425	24	______	______
6. D2-0463	2	______	______
7. E2-0467	20	______	______

Product Code	# Received	Updated # on Hand	Updated Inventory Cost
8. G1-0178	4	________	________________
9. G4-0257	6	________	________________
10. H2-0327	12	________	________________

NAME ______________________

DATE ______________________

SCORE ______________________

PROJECT FIVE

NEW AGE OFFICE SUPPLY

ASSIGNMENT 34 DELETE PRODUCTS FROM THE INVENTORY FILE

omit

New Age Office Supply has decided to discontinue selling five of the products in its inventory file because the products have not sold well. Because there is no remaining stock on hand or on order, you have been asked to delete the records for the five products. Use the information below to delete the records, and document the deletions by writing your initials in the Record Deleted By column.

Product Code and Description		Record Deleted By
1. B3-0344	DATA CART	**1.** ______________
2. B3-0398	MOBILE SECURITY CABINET	**2.** ______________
3. D2-0453	VISIBLE FILE 10 TRAY	**3.** ______________
4. E3-0237	MAG TAPE CARRYING CASE	**4.** ______________
5. G4-0344	STANDING DIRECTORY BOARD	**5.** ______________

NAME ____________________

DATE ____________________

SCORE ____________________

PROJECT FIVE

NEW AGE OFFICE SUPPLY

ASSIGNMENT 35 ADD PRODUCTS TO THE INVENTORY FILE

omit.

New Age Office Supply frequently adds new items to its product line. The forms below contain information about ten new products that have been received. Add the ten new products to the file. Because these are products for which there is no former "on hand" amount, your entry in the On Hand field will be the number received. Compute and enter in your computer file the amount for the Inventory Cost field. Finally, to document the additions, write the inventory cost in the space provided on each form.

PRODUCT CODE: A1-0194 DESCRIPTION: MICROCOMPUTER CENTER

SUPPLIER: Data Case Enterprises

UNIT COST: $94.50 SELLING PRICE: $175.00

RECEIVED: 6 INVENTORY COST: ____________________

PRODUCT CODE: B1-0127 DESCRIPTION: ROLLING FILE

SUPPLIER: Steel Furniture Company

UNIT COST: $83.50 SELLING PRICE: $144.00

RECEIVED: 4 INVENTORY COST: ____________________

PRODUCT CODE: B3-0327 DESCRIPTION: MOBILE DATA UNIT

SUPPLIER: DCR Business Equipment

UNIT COST: $80.60 SELLING PRICE: $139.00

RECEIVED: 12 INVENTORY COST: ____________________

PRODUCT CODE: D2-0488 DESCRIPTION: PORTABLE VISIBLE FILE

SUPPLIER: Torrence File Products

UNIT COST: $51.90 SELLING PRICE: $92.80

RECEIVED: 24 INVENTORY COST: ____________________

PRODUCT CODE: E1-0289 DESCRIPTION: CONTINENTAL ATTACHE

SUPPLIER: United Luggage

UNIT COST: $39.00 SELLING PRICE: $75.00

RECEIVED: 12 INVENTORY COST: ____________________

PRODUCT CODE: E2-0411 DESCRIPTION: EASY OPEN PORTFOLIO

SUPPLIER: Fancini Products

UNIT COST: $8.10 SELLING PRICE: $15.50

RECEIVED: 36 INVENTORY COST: ____________________

PRODUCT CODE: F1-0147 DESCRIPTION: COMPACT DISK STAPLER

SUPPLIER: Romero Manufacturing Co.

UNIT COST: $5.90 SELLING PRICE: $8.95

RECEIVED: 60 INVENTORY COST: ____________________

PRODUCT CODE: G4-0242 DESCRIPTION: TELESCOPING POINTER

SUPPLIER: Romero Manufacturing Co.

UNIT COST: $2.10 SELLING PRICE: $3.50

RECEIVED: 24 INVENTORY COST: ____________________

PRODUCT CODE: H1-0323 DESCRIPTION: DESK ORGANIZER

SUPPLIER: Quality Office Systems

UNIT COST: $3.05 SELLING PRICE: $5.50

RECEIVED: 60 INVENTORY COST: ____________________

PRODUCT CODE: H4-0150 DESCRIPTION: PAPER SHREDDER

SUPPLIER: East Coast Mfg. Company

UNIT COST: $304.95 SELLING PRICE: $449.00

RECEIVED: 2 INVENTORY COST: ____________________

NAME ____________________

DATE ____________________

SCORE ____________________

PROJECT FIVE

NEW AGE OFFICE SUPPLY

ASSIGNMENT 36 MAKE PRICE AND COST CHANGES IN THE INVENTORY FILE

omit

In order to keep the inventory file up to date, changes in prices and costs must frequently be made. A change in the unit cost of a product, as you have already seen, also changes the inventory cost. However, if New Age Office Supply raises or lowers its selling price of a product, the inventory cost does not change. This is because inventory cost is based on unit cost, not selling price. Use the information below to change unit cost and selling price amounts in your computer file. For any change in a unit cost, also compute and record in your computer file an updated inventory cost based upon the number of items on hand. Document that you have made each change by writing the product description for changes in selling price and updated inventory cost for changes in unit cost in the space provided. An example is given at the beginning of the listing of each type of change.

Product Code	Change in Selling Price	Product Description
0. A2-0299	Reduce to $542.00	**0.** LATERAL FILE
1. A2-0476	Increase by $12.00	**1.** ____________
2. A4-0421	Reduce by $8.00	**2.** ____________
3. B3-0266	Increase to $51.90	**3.** ____________
4. C2-0235	Reduce to $37.95	**4.** ____________
5. D1-0212	Increase by $1.45	**5.** ____________
6. D2-0368	Reduce by $3.30	**6.** ____________
7. E1-0255	Increase to $192.50	**7.** ____________
8. F1-0332	Reduce to $119.75	**8.** ____________
9. F3-0179	Increase by 10%	**9.** ____________
10. G3-0155	Decrease by 15%	**10.** ____________

Product Code	Change in Unit Cost	Updated Inventory Cost
0. A2-0358	Increase to $301.86	**0.** $905.58
1. A3-0478	Reduce by $8.80	**1.**
2. B3-0189	Reduce to $119.87	**2.**
3. C1-0153	Increase to $16.10	**3.**
4. D1-0366	Reduce by $3.20	**4.**
5. E1-0220	Increase by $3.12	**5.**
6. E2-0543	Increase to $12.79	**6.**
7. F1-0212	Reduce to $2.05	**7.**
8. G1-0236	Increase by $12.00	**8.**
9. G3-0397	Reduce by 15%	**9.**
10. H1-0413	Increase by 10%	**10.**

NAME ______________

DATE ______________

SCORE ______________

PROJECT FIVE

NEW AGE OFFICE SUPPLY

ASSIGNMENT 37 RETRIEVE INVENTORY INFORMATION

As the person responsible for the inventory file at New Age Office Supply, you are frequently asked questions about individual products as well as categories of products. For each of the following requests, retrieve the information and write your response in the space provided. An example is given.

0. What is the description of product code A2-0523? **0.** POSTURE CHAIR

✓ **1.** Who is the supplier of product code B3-0313? **1.** D & R Business Equipment

✓ **2.** What is the product code for the ergonomic chair? **2.** A3-0421

✓ **3.** What are the number on hand and inventory cost of product code D2-0177? **3.** 11, 183.59

✓ **4.** What are the unit cost and selling price of product code C2-0273? **4.** 17.96, 28.50

✓ **5.** What are the unit cost and number on hand for the visible frame 12 × 8? **5.** 14.11, 6.

✓ **6.** What is the gross margin for the presentation easel (see Assignment ~~1~~ 31, Question 7)? **6.** 70.56

✓ **7.** How many different products in the inventory file have Visual Display, Inc. as the supplier? **7.** 21

✓ **8.** For how many different products is the number on hand fewer than four? **8.** 22

✓ **9.** What are the product codes of all products priced to sell at more than $700.00? A2-0158, A2-0267, D2-0463, G1-0138

✓ **10.** What are the descriptions for each product having an inventory cost greater than $5,000.00?

Task Chair, Economy stacking chair, stacking chair, 4 Drawer Lateral File

✓ **11.** What are the descriptions for each product supplied by Fancini Products for which the number on hand is fewer than 10? Blueprint shears, Editors shears, Executive meeting Case, Slim Catalog Case, Ziparound Portfolio

✓ **12.** What are the descriptions for all products which have the word *PORTFOLIO* in the description?

Budget Portfolio, Easy Open Portfolio, Slim underarm portfolio, Tri-pocket Portfolio, Ziparound portfolio

✓ **13.** How many descriptions begin with the letters *DESK?* (This includes words such as *DESKTOP*.) **13.** 8

✓ **14.** What are the product codes of all products supplied by Romero Manufacturing Co. for which our unit cost is between $50.00 and $100.00? C2-0246, D1-0366, F1-0332, G4-0136, G4-0288

✓ **15.** How many products have a selling price greater than $200.00 *and* a number on hand greater than nine? **15.** 13

✓ **16.** What is the total of the inventory costs for all products supplied by Eskay Lighting, Inc.? **16.** 6352.38

17. A customer wants to purchase two of product code A3-0279, workstation chair, and three of product code B3-0266, desktop file. What is the total of the selling prices of the five items? **17.** ______

18. Refer to Question 17, above. The sales manager decided to give the customer a 10 percent discount on the chairs and a 15 percent discount on the files. What is the total discounted selling price? **18.** ______

19. What is the average selling price of all products supplied by Torrence File Products? 19. 171.80

20. How many different products does New Age Office Supply have listed in its inventory file? 20. 205

Bonus Problems

1. What is the total inventory cost of all products in the inventory file? 1. ~~18731.14~~ 187931.14

2. What would the total inventory cost be if all unit costs were decreased by 5 percent? 2. ~~197327.70~~ 178 534.58

NAME ____________

DATE ____________

SCORE ____________

PROJECT FIVE

NEW AGE OFFICE SUPPLY

ASSIGNMENT 38 PRINT INVENTORY INFORMATION

In this assignment, you will use the inventory file of New Age Office Supply to print information about the company's products. After completing each printing job, answer any questions related to it in the space provided.

✓**1a.** Print a list of the product codes, descriptions, and unit costs for all products supplied by Eskay Lighting, Inc. Arrange the list by product code.

1b. How many products are on the list? **1b.** 9

✓**2a.** Print a list of product codes, unit costs, and inventory cost for all products with a unit cost greater than $200.00. Arrange the list in descending order by unit cost.

✓**2b.** What is the highest unit cost on the list? **2b.** 665.84

2c. What is the lowest unit cost on the list? **2c.** 207.00

3a. Print a list of product codes, suppliers, and number on hand for all products having fewer than three on hand. Arrange the list in order by name of supplier.

✓**3b.** How many different suppliers are on the list? **3b.** 8

Bonus Problems

1. Design bin labels (you may use self-adhesive mailing labels) to be used to mark the shelf location of various products in the warehouse. Do not include unit cost, number on hand, or inventory cost on the labels. Print one label for each product whose code begins with C1. 8 labels

2. Print a report showing the gross margin for each product. Arrange the report in order by product code, and include the product code, unit cost, and selling price. Add appropriate headings if your software allows.

3. Note that each product code begins with a letter of the alphabet, *A* through *H*. Determine the number of different products in each of these lettered categories. Prepare a pie chart (circle graph) showing the number of different products in each of the eight lettered categories. Add appropriate captions and legends as allowed by your software.

4. Prepare a bar graph comparing unit cost and selling price for each of the following products: D1-0137, E2-0543, F1-0422, and G2-0215.

NAME ____________________

DATE ____________________

SCORE ____________________

PROJECT FIVE

NEW AGE OFFICE SUPPLY

ASSIGNMENT 39 PROJECT QUIZ

Before you take this quiz, you should have completed the previous assignments so that your inventory file will be completely updated. You will use the inventory file at your computer to answer the questions.

1. How many products in the file are supplied by Fancini Products? **1.** 20

2. Update your inventory file as a result of a sale of three economy tabletop easels. What is the updated number on hand? **2.** 11

Calculated field

3. Update your inventory file as a result of the receipt of one conference wall cabinet. What is the updated inventory cost? **3.** $894.00

omit

4a. What is the selling price of product F3-0288? **4a.** 17.00

4b. Increase this selling price by 10 percent in your inventory file. What is the increased selling price? **4b.** 18.70

calculated field

5a. What is the description of product code E1-0230? **5a.** Perfecto Leather Attache

5b. Delete this product from the inventory file, and document the deletion by writing your initials. **5b.** RA

6. Add a new product to the inventory file using the information on the form below. Write the inventory cost of the new product in the space provided. Omit

```
PRODUCT CODE:  G3-0462      DESCRIPTION:  REVERSIBLE CHALKBOARD
SUPPLIER:  Visual Display Inc.
UNIT COST:  $124.80         SELLING PRICE:  $208.00
# RECEIVED:  3              INVENTORY COST: ____________________
```

7. What is the gross margin for product B3-0189? calculated field — 7. ~~Total 4906.25~~ individual 98.01

8. How many cantilever chairs are on hand? — 8. 4

9. What are the descriptions of all products supplied by Visual Display, Inc. that sell for more than $200.00? chalkboard 42x60, chalkboard 48x72, Dry erase board 4'x6', stowaway board easel

10. Print a list of the 10 products in the file having the highest selling price. Include product code, description, and selling price. Arrange the list in descending order by selling price. What is the last price on the list? Attach the list to this quiz and give it to your instructor. — 10. ______

highest = 1189.
lowest = 537.95
(min) desending sort.

Project Five (Printout of Database After Completion of All Assignments Except Quiz)

	PRODUCT CODE	DESCRIPTION	SUPPLIER
1.	A1-0135	MICROCOMPUTER TABLE	Data Case Enterprises
2.	A1-0157	MICROCOMPUTER STAND	Data Case Enterprises
3.	A1-0194	MICROCOMPUTER CENTER	Data Case Enterprises
4.	A1-0233	BI-LEVEL COMPUTER STAND	Steel Furniture Company
5.	A1-0252	PAPER CATCH BASKET	Steel Furniture Company
6.	A1-0276	ADJUSTABLE TERMINAL TABLE	Superior Office Products
7.	A1-0310	MOBILE TERMINAL TABLE	Romero Manufacturing Co.
8.	A1-0327	PRINTER STAND	Data Case Enterprises
9.	A1-0359	PAPER FEED TRAY	Steel Furniture Company
10.	A2-0188	EXECUTIVE DESK	Steel Furniture Company
11.	A2-0267	CREDENZA	Steel Furniture Company
12.	A2-0299	LATERAL FILE	Steel Furniture Company
13.	A2-0315	ADMINISTRATIVE DESK	DCR Business Equipment
14.	A2-0334	COMPACT DESK	DCR Business Equipment
15.	A2-0358	WORK CENTER	DCR Business Equipment
16.	A2-0377	CONFERENCE DESK	Superior Office Products
17.	A2-0425	EXECUTIVE SWIVEL CHAIR	Superior Office Products
18.	A2-0476	CONFERENCE CHAIR	Superior Office Products
19.	A2-0523	POSTURE CHAIR	DCR Business Equipment
20.	A3-0256	TASK CHAIR	Superior Office Products
21.	A3-0279	WORKSTATION CHAIR	Steel Furniture Company
22.	A3-0344	PNEUMATIC TASK CHAIR	Steel Furniture Company
23.	A3-0421	ERGONOMIC CHAIR	Steel Furniture Company
24.	A3-0478	CANTILEVER CHAIR	Steel Furniture Company
25.	A3-0525	SIDE CHAIR	Steel Furniture Company
26.	A3-0589	ARMLESS PULL UP CHAIR	Steel Furniture Company
27.	A3-0614	GUEST ARM CHAIR	Steel Furniture Company
28.	A3-0637	STENO POSTURE CHAIR	Steel Furniture Company
29.	A4-0113	SPRING BACK STOOL	Superior Office Products
30.	A4-0179	BACKLESS ROUND SEAT STOOL	Superior Office Products
31.	A4-0222	PNEUMATIC-LIFT STOOL	Superior Office Products
32.	A4-0343	DESIGNER STOOL	Superior Office Products
33.	A4-0356	STEEL FOLDING CHAIR	Romero Manufacturing Co.
34.	A4-0389	ECONOMY STACKING CHAIR	Romero Manufacturing Co.
35.	A4-0421	STACKING CHAIR	Romero Manufacturing Co.
36.	A4-0488	SLED BASE STACKING CHAIR	Romero Manufacturing Co.
37.	A4-0523	STEP STOOL	Romero Manufacturing Co.
38.	A4-0544	MOBILE FILING STOOL	Romero Manufacturing Co.
39.	B1-0127	ROLLING FILE	Steel Furniture Company
40.	B1-0156	5 DRAWER FILE, LETTER	Steel Furniture Company
41.	B1-0166	5 DRAWER FILE, LEGAL	Steel Furniture Company
42.	B1-0176	4 DRAWER FILE, LETTER	Steel Furniture Company
43.	B1-0186	4 DRAWER FILE, LEGAL	Steel Furniture Company
44.	B1-0196	3 DRAWER FILE, LETTER	Steel Furniture Company
45.	B1-0206	3 DRAWER FILE, LEGAL	Steel Furniture Company
46.	B1-0216	2 DRAWER FILE, LETTER	Steel Furniture Company
47.	B1-0226	2 DRAWER FILE, LEGAL	Steel Furniture Company
48.	B2-0135	WOOD LATERAL FILE	Steel Furniture Company
49.	B2-0174	4 DRAWER LATERAL FILE	Steel Furniture Company
50.	B2-0184	3 DRAWER LATERAL FILE	Steel Furniture Company
51.	B2-0194	2 DRAWER LATERAL FILE	Steel Furniture Company
52.	B3-0153	DESK SIDE MOBILE FILE	DCR Business Equipment
53.	B3-0189	PRINTOUT MOBILE FILE	DCR Business Equipment
54.	B3-0236	MOBILE PEDESTAL AND FILE	DCR Business Equipment
55.	B3-0266	DESKTOP FILE	DCR Business Equipment

	PRODUCT CODE	DESCRIPTION	SUPPLIER
56.	B3-0313	MAIL/DATA CART	DCR Business Equipment
57.	B3-0327	MOBILE DATA UNIT	DCR Business Equipment
58.	B3-0379	4 WAY DATA RACK	DCR Business Equipment
59.	B4-0111	PKG DOCUMATE CARTRIDGES	Fancini Products
60.	B4-0154	PKG DOCUMATE BINDERS	Fancini Products
61.	B4-0177	PKG BINDER COVERS	Fancini Products
62.	B4-0285	PKG DOCUMATE FOLDERS	Fancini Products
63.	C1-0114	TELEPHONE INDEX	Superior Office Products
64.	C1-0153	TELEPHONE LIST FINDER	Superior Office Products
65.	C1-0246	TELEPHONE SHOULDER REST	Superior Office Products
66.	C1-0277	TELEPHONE HEADSET	Superior Office Products
67.	C1-0317	MINI PHONE SHOULDER REST	DCR Business Equipment
68.	C1-0368	PHONE CUSHION	DCR Business Equipment
69.	C1-0385	PHONE LOCK	DCR Business Equipment
70.	C1-0422	MESSAGE HOLDER	DCR Business Equipment
71.	C2-0235	CASH BOX	Romero Manufacturing Co.
72.	C2-0246	CASH DRAWER	Romero Manufacturing Co.
73.	C2-0273	COLOR-KEYED COIN TUBE SET	Romero Manufacturing Co.
74.	C2-0349	COUNTER CHANGE TRAY	Romero Manufacturing Co.
75.	C2-0388	DEEP COIN TRAY	Romero Manufacturing Co.
76.	C2-0398	SHALLOW COIN TRAY	Romero Manufacturing Co.
77.	D1-0124	BUSINESS CARD FILE	Data Case Enterprises
78.	D1-0137	DESKTOP TRAY FILE	Data Case Enterprises
79.	D1-0168	DESKTOP VUE FILE	Data Case Enterprises
80.	D1-0212	COVERED VUE FILE	Data Case Enterprises
81.	D1-0225	COVERED SWIVEL FILE	Data Case Enterprises
82.	D1-0264	ROTARY CARD FILE 2.25 x 4	Visual Display Inc.
83.	D1-0274	ROTARY CARD FILE 3 x 5	Visual Display Inc.
84.	D1-0284	ROTARY CARD FILE 4 x 6	Visual Display Inc.
85.	D1-0323	DATA FILE 2.25 x 4	Data Case Enterprises
86.	D1-0333	DATA FILE 3 x 5	Data Case Enterprises
87.	D1-0366	TWIN ROTARY CARD FILE	Romero Manufacturing Co.
88.	D1-0425	CLOSED ROTARY FILE	Romero Manufacturing Co.
89.	D2-0147	VISIBLE FRAME 12 x 6	Torrence File Products
90.	D2-0157	VISIBLE FRAME 12 x 8	Torrence File Products
91.	D2-0167	VISIBLE FRAME 20 x 6	Torrence File Products
92.	D2-0177	VISIBLE FRAME 20 x 8	Torrence File Products
93.	D2-0222	FRAME HOUSING 12 INCH	Torrence File Products
94.	D2-0232	FRAME HOUSING 20 INCH	Torrence File Products
95.	D2-0246	VISIBLE UNIT BOOK 5 x 3	Torrence File Products
96.	D2-0256	VISIBLE UNIT BOOK 6 x 4	Torrence File Products
97.	D2-0266	VISIBLE UNIT BOOK 8 x 5	Torrence File Products
98.	D2-0368	VISIBLE RECORD FOLDER	Torrence File Products
99.	D2-0389	VISIBLE RECORD BOOK	Torrence File Products
100.	D2-0443	VISIBLE FILE 5 TRAY	Torrence File Products
101.	D2-0463	VISIBLE FILE 17 TRAY	Torrence File Products
102.	D2-0488	PORTABLE VISIBLE FILE	Torrence File Products
103.	E1-0168	RENWAY VINYL ATTACHE	United Luggage
104.	E1-0220	PERFECTO TWEED ATTACHE	United Luggage
105.	E1-0230	PERFECTO LEATHER ATTACHE	United Luggage
106.	E1-0245	ULTIMA VINYL ATTACHE	United Luggage
107.	E1-0255	ULTIMA TWEED ATTACHE	United Luggage
108.	E1-0265	ULTIMA LEATHER ATTACHE	United Luggage
109.	E1-0289	CONTINENTAL ATTACHE	United Luggage
110.	E2-0233	LEATHER UNDERARM ENVELOPE	Fancini Products
111.	E2-0258	SLIM UNDERARM PORTFOLIO	Fancini Products

	PRODUCT CODE	DESCRIPTION	SUPPLIER
112.	E2-0348	ZIPAROUND PORTFOLIO	Fancini Products
113.	E2-0399	TRI-POCKET PORTFOLIO	Fancini Products
114.	E2-0411	EASY OPEN PORTFOLIO	Fancini Products
115.	E2-0425	EXECUTIVE MEETING CASE	Fancini Products
116.	E2-0467	CATALOG CASE	Fancini Products
117.	E2-0478	SLIM CATALOG CASE	Fancini Products
118.	E2-0512	EXECUTIVE BRIEF BAG	Fancini Products
119.	E2-0543	BUDGET PORTFOLIO	Fancini Products
120.	E3-0174	EXPANDING ENVELOPE	United Luggage
121.	E3-0198	CARTRIDGE CARRYING CASE	Data Case Enterprises
122.	E3-0258	DISK PACK CARRYING CASE	Data Case Enterprises
123.	E3-0346	COMPACT LUGGAGE CARRIER	Data Case Enterprises
124.	F1-0133	DESK STAPLER	Romero Manufacturing Co.
125.	F1-0147	COMPACT DESK STAPLER	Romero Manufacturing Co.
126.	F1-0167	CUSTOM DESK STAPLER	Romero Manufacturing Co.
127.	F1-0212	STAPLE REMOVER	Romero Manufacturing Co.
128.	F1-0244	HALF STRIP STAPLER	Romero Manufacturing Co.
129.	F1-0278	HAND PLIER STAPLER	Romero Manufacturing Co.
130.	F1-0298	CONTOUR PLIER STAPLER	Romero Manufacturing Co.
131.	F1-0332	ELECTRIC STAPLER	Romero Manufacturing Co.
132.	F1-0342	CUSTOM ELECTRIC STAPLER	Romero Manufacturing Co.
133.	F1-0352	HEAVY DUTY STAPLER	Romero Manufacturing Co.
134.	F1-0399	HEAVY DUTY GUN TACKER	Romero Manufacturing Co.
135.	F1-0422	HI COMPRESSION STAPLE GUN	Romero Manufacturing Co.
136.	F2-0144	3-HOLE PUNCH	Superior Office Products
137.	F2-0163	HEAVY DUTY HOLE PUNCH	Superior Office Products
138.	F2-0177	SINGLE HOLE HAND PUNCH	Superior Office Products
139.	F2-0213	2-HOLE ECONOMY PUNCH	Superior Office Products
140.	F2-0254	CUSTOM 2-HOLE PUNCH	Superior Office Products
141.	F3-0135	EDITORS SHEARS	Fancini Products
142.	F3-0158	BLUEPRINT SHEARS	Fancini Products
143.	F3-0179	STRAIGHT TRIMMERS	Fancini Products
144.	F3-0237	STATIONERS SHEARS	Fancini Products
145.	F3-0288	LEFTY STRAIGHT TRIMMERS	Fancini Products
146.	F3-0345	LIGHTWEIGHT POWER SNIPS	Fancini Products
147.	G1-0138	CONFERENCE WALL CABINET	DCR Business Equipment
148.	G1-0155	VISUAL AID CABINET	DCR Business Equipment
149.	G1-0178	MAGNETIC VISUAL BOARD	DCR Business Equipment
150.	G1-0236	REVERSIBLE BOARD	DCR Business Equipment
151.	G1-0257	DRY ERASE BOARD 2' x 3'	Visual Display Inc.
152.	G1-0267	DRY ERASE BOARD 3' x 4'	Visual Display Inc.
153.	G1-0277	DRY ERASE BOARD 4' x 6'	Visual Display Inc.
154.	G2-0179	FABRIC TACKBOARD 2' x 3'	Visual Display Inc.
155.	G2-0189	FABRIC TACKBOARD 3' x 4'	Visual Display Inc.
156.	G2-0215	CORK TACKBOARD 1' x 3'	Visual Display Inc.
157.	G2-0225	CORK TACKBOARD 2' x 3'	Visual Display Inc.
158.	G2-0235	CORK TACKBOARD 3' x 4'	Visual Display Inc.
159.	G2-0245	CORK TACKBOARD 4' x 6'	Visual Display Inc.
160.	G3-0155	SCHEDULE PLANNER	Superior Office Products
161.	G3-0189	MONTHLY PLANNER	Superior Office Products
162.	G3-0236	FOUR-MONTH PLANNER	Superior Office Products
163.	G3-0268	CONTOUR MESSAGE CENTER	Visual Display Inc.
164.	G3-0314	STOW AWAY BOARD EASEL	Visual Display Inc.
165.	G3-0356	PORCELAIN STEEL BOARD	Visual Display Inc.
166.	G3-0397	PRESENTATION EASEL	Visual Display Inc.
167.	G3-0424	CHALKBOARD 36 x 48	Visual Display Inc.

	PRODUCT CODE	DESCRIPTION	SUPPLIER
168.	G3-0434	CHALKBOARD 42 x 60	Visual Display Inc.
169.	G3-0444	CHALKBOARD 48 x 72	Visual Display Inc.
170.	G3-0479	TELESCOPING EASEL	Visual Display Inc.
171.	G3-0514	ECONOMY TABLETOP EASEL	Visual Display Inc.
172.	G4-0136	CONTROL MESSAGE CENTER	Romero Manufacturing Co.
173.	G4-0160	CHANGEABLE LETTER BOARD	Romero Manufacturing Co.
174.	G4-0224	BULLETIN BOARD 3' x 4'	Romero Manufacturing Co.
175.	G4-0234	BULLETIN BOARD 3' x 5'	Romero Manufacturing Co.
176.	G4-0242	TELESCOPING POINTER	Romero Manufacturing Co.
177.	G4-0247	DIRECTORY BOARD 3' x 4'	Romero Manufacturing Co.
178.	G4-0257	DIRECTORY BOARD 3' x 5'	Romero Manufacturing Co.
179.	G4-0288	ENCLOSED CORK BOARD	Romero Manufacturing Co.
180.	H1-0135	PENCIL CUP	Quality Office Systems
181.	H1-0153	DESK PAD 20 x 34	Quality Office Systems
182.	H1-0163	DESK PAD 24 x 36	Quality Office Systems
183.	H1-0226	LETTER TRAY	Quality Office Systems
184.	H1-0254	MEMO HOLDER	Quality Office Systems
185.	H1-0279	CALENDAR HOLDER	Quality Office Systems
186.	H1-0314	SIDE-LOAD STACKABLE TRAY	Quality Office Systems
187.	H1-0323	DESK ORGANIZER	Quality Office Systems
188.	H1-0348	BOOKENDS	Quality Office Systems
189.	H1-0378	TAPE DISPENSER	Quality Office Systems
190.	H1-0413	CLIP DISPENSER	Quality Office Systems
191.	H1-0429	PEN SET	Quality Office Systems
192.	H1-0462	WASTEBASKET	Quality Office Systems
193.	H2-0132	TRADITIONAL DESK LAMP	Eskay Lighting Inc.
194.	H2-0150	GOOSENECK DESK LAMP	Eskay Lighting Inc.
195.	H2-0186	HIGH INTENSITY DESK LAMP	Eskay Lighting Inc.
196.	H2-0218	CONTEMPORARY CLIP LIGHT	Eskay Lighting Inc.
197.	H2-0245	CLAMP-ON EXTENSION LAMP	Eskay Lighting Inc.
198.	H2-0275	ASYMMETRIC LAMP	Eskay Lighting Inc.
199.	H2-0327	MAGNIFYING DESK LAMP	Eskay Lighting Inc.
200.	H2-0359	CLAMP-ON FLUORESCENT LAMP	Eskay Lighting Inc.
201.	H2-0388	COMPUTER LAMP	Eskay Lighting Inc.
202.	H3-0148	SURGE PROTECTOR	Data Case Enterprises
203.	H3-0167	SURGE PROTECTOR W/ FILTER	Data Case Enterprises
204.	H3-0235	POWER STRIP	Data Case Enterprises
205.	H4-0150	PAPER SHREDDER	East Coast Mfg. Company

	UNIT COST	SELLING PRICE	ON HAND	INVENTORY COST
1.	150.66	279.00	12	1,807.92
2.	48.06	89.00	6	288.36
3.	94.50	175.00	6	567.00
4.	83.70	155.00	7	585.90
5.	15.12	28.00	2	30.24
6.	157.95	292.50	3	473.85
7.	112.86	209.00	11	1,241.46
8.	90.45	167.50	7	633.15
9.	18.63	34.50	8	149.04
10.	463.86	859.00	4	1,855.44
11.	399.33	739.50	2	798.66
12.	292.68	542.00	15	4,390.20
13.	188.46	349.00	2	376.92
14.	143.91	266.50	6	863.46
15.	301.86	559.00	3	905.58
16.	306.72	568.00	2	613.44
17.	149.58	277.00	7	1,047.06
18.	100.98	199.00	36	3,635.28
19.	129.06	239.00	17	2,194.02
20.	72.63	134.50	140	10,168.20
21.	57.78	107.00	20	1,155.60
22.	68.58	127.00	5	342.90
23.	194.27	359.75	6	1,165.62
24.	102.17	205.50	4	408.68
25.	161.87	299.75	18	2,913.66
26.	74.36	137.70	11	817.96
27.	83.65	154.90	14	1,171.10
28.	107.84	199.70	21	2,264.64
29.	71.52	132.45	4	286.08
30.	51.00	94.45	14	714.00
31.	129.41	239.65	6	776.46
32.	160.49	297.20	8	1,283.92
33.	13.88	25.70	48	666.24
34.	18.23	33.75	340	6,198.20
35.	33.64	54.30	212	7,131.68
36.	47.36	87.70	91	4,309.76
37.	26.19	48.50	6	157.14
38.	28.84	53.40	14	403.76
39.	83.50	144.00	4	334.00
40.	190.82	329.00	14	2,671.48
41.	210.54	363.00	23	4,842.42
42.	137.46	237.00	14	1,924.44
43.	157.76	272.00	8	1,262.08
44.	115.42	199.00	7	807.94
45.	138.62	239.00	2	277.24
46.	98.02	169.00	12	1,176.24
47.	144.84	198.00	3	434.52
48.	211.70	365.00	5	1,058.50
49.	405.86	699.75	27	10,958.22
50.	312.01	537.95	9	2,808.09
51.	242.41	417.95	4	969.64
52.	74.44	128.35	8	595.52
53.	119.87	217.88	5	599.35
54.	172.84	298.00	4	691.36
55.	28.71	51.90	18	516.78

	UNIT COST	SELLING PRICE	ON HAND	INVENTORY COST
56.	168.17	289.95	2	336.34
57.	80.60	139.00	12	967.20
58.	118.61	204.50	2	237.22
59.	6.24	10.75	400	2,496.00
60.	8.26	14.25	150	1,239.00
61.	2.61	4.50	182	475.02
62.	3.34	5.75	214	714.76
63.	13.39	21.25	27	361.53
64.	16.10	22.70	18	289.80
65.	6.23	9.89	34	211.82
66.	18.87	29.95	15	283.05
67.	3.40	5.39	17	57.80
68.	1.00	1.59	77	77.00
69.	4.00	6.35	15	60.00
70.	2.32	3.69	196	454.72
71.	24.54	37.95	12	294.48
72.	99.86	158.50	3	299.58
73.	17.96	28.50	9	161.64
74.	22.52	35.75	36	810.72
75.	5.01	7.95	8	40.08
76.	3.50	5.55	40	140.00
77.	10.05	17.95	68	683.40
78.	10.36	18.50	55	569.80
79.	9.07	16.20	10	90.70
80.	13.86	26.20	16	221.76
81.	20.13	35.95	19	382.47
82.	16.10	28.75	30	483.00
83.	18.45	32.95	14	258.30
84.	53.06	94.75	21	1,114.26
85.	10.63	18.98	24	255.12
86.	12.25	21.88	16	196.00
87.	52.66	99.75	40	2,106.40
88.	20.69	36.95	24	496.56
89.	13.27	23.70	8	106.16
90.	14.11	25.20	6	84.66
91.	15.29	27.30	5	76.45
92.	16.69	29.80	11	183.59
93.	92.68	165.50	6	556.08
94.	92.68	165.50	3	278.04
95.	36.51	65.20	20	730.20
96.	37.69	67.30	16	603.04
97.	37.91	67.70	13	492.83
98.	11.14	16.60	8	89.12
99.	16.66	29.75	41	683.06
100.	246.34	439.90	2	492.68
101.	665.84	1,189.00	2	1,331.68
102.	51.90	92.80	24	1,245.60
103.	34.06	65.50	21	715.26
104.	59.80	109.00	21	1,255.80
105.	91.00	175.00	26	2,366.00
106.	58.24	112.00	16	931.84
107.	97.50	192.50	19	1,852.50
108.	111.77	214.95	17	1,900.09
109.	39.00	75.00	12	468.00
110.	18.98	36.50	20	379.60
111.	29.48	56.70	10	294.80

	UNIT COST	SELLING PRICE	ON HAND	INVENTORY COST
112.	54.44	104.70	8	435.52
113.	58.24	112.00	31	1,805.44
114.	8.10	15.50	36	291.60
115.	48.88	94.00	7	342.16
116.	43.16	83.00	22	949.52
117.	40.04	77.00	6	240.24
118.	33.54	64.50	14	469.56
119.	12.79	19.40	13	166.27
120.	4.76	9.15	10	47.60
121.	41.55	79.90	6	249.30
122.	74.10	142.50	5	370.50
123.	16.64	32.00	6	99.84
124.	12.05	18.25	31	373.55
125.	5.90	8.95	60	354.00
126.	15.81	23.95	27	426.87
127.	2.05	3.40	193	395.65
128.	8.38	12.70	107	896.66
129.	10.03	15.20	68	682.04
130.	8.18	12.40	27	220.86
131.	82.47	119.75	40	3,298.80
132.	135.93	205.95	18	2,446.74
133.	31.28	47.40	9	281.52
134.	15.11	22.90	19	287.09
135.	11.85	17.95	23	272.55
136.	30.62	46.40	14	428.68
137.	61.22	92.75	11	673.42
138.	11.19	16.95	51	570.69
139.	5.58	8.45	15	83.70
140.	28.22	42.75	13	366.86
141.	13.17	19.95	9	118.53
142.	14.65	22.20	4	58.60
143.	11.22	18.70	77	863.94
144.	11.55	17.50	16	184.80
145.	11.22	17.00	26	291.72
146.	5.21	7.90	34	177.14
147.	447.00	745.00	1	447.00
148.	288.00	480.00	7	2,016.00
149.	149.40	249.00	5	747.00
150.	339.00	545.00	5	1,695.00
151.	52.77	87.95	16	844.32
152.	86.97	144.95	14	1,217.58
153.	161.37	268.95	11	1,775.07
154.	25.80	43.00	17	438.60
155.	40.50	67.50	18	729.00
156.	13.80	23.00	20	276.00
157.	17.40	29.00	19	330.60
158.	29.70	49.50	19	564.30
159.	57.00	95.00	2	114.00
160.	37.80	53.55	7	264.60
161.	37.80	63.00	4	151.20
162.	37.80	63.00	2	75.60
163.	6.30	10.50	48	302.40
164.	135.00	225.00	6	810.00
165.	85.20	142.00	2	170.40
166.	73.44	144.00	7	514.08
167.	105.00	175.00	6	630.00

	UNIT COST	SELLING PRICE	ON HAND	INVENTORY COST
168.	129.00	215.00	5	645.00
169.	153.00	255.00	6	918.00
170.	25.50	42.50	4	102.00
171.	8.85	14.75	14	123.90
172.	69.60	116.00	17	1,183.20
173.	22.20	37.00	5	111.00
174.	171.00	285.00	1	171.00
175.	207.00	345.00	3	621.00
176.	2.10	3.50	24	50.40
177.	186.00	310.00	6	1,116.00
178.	212.40	354.00	10	2,124.00
179.	77.40	129.00	5	387.00
180.	2.74	4.99	44	120.56
181.	14.29	25.98	27	385.83
182.	16.49	29.98	24	395.76
183.	4.89	8.89	27	132.03
184.	3.84	6.99	8	30.72
185.	3.84	6.99	31	119.04
186.	4.67	8.49	26	121.42
187.	3.05	5.50	60	183.00
188.	6.59	11.98	40	263.60
189.	7.96	14.48	42	334.32
190.	1.98	3.28	50	99.00
191.	9.34	16.98	19	177.46
192.	9.34	16.98	38	354.92
193.	30.22	54.95	26	785.72
194.	24.17	43.95	16	386.72
195.	19.24	34.98	15	288.60
196.	8.55	15.55	17	145.35
197.	25.30	46.00	2	50.60
198.	48.95	89.00	7	342.65
199.	70.95	129.00	15	1,064.25
200.	63.22	114.95	17	1,074.74
201.	63.25	115.00	35	2,213.75
202.	17.02	30.95	119	2,025.38
203.	26.37	47.95	84	2,215.08
204.	8.77	15.95	276	2,420.52
205.	304.95	449.00	2	609.90

Project Six (Printout of Database After Completion of All Assignments Except Quiz)

	LAST NAME	FIRST NAME	M.I.	SOCIAL SECURITY NO.	PHONE
1.	Abbott	Jane	T.	309-22-8351	305-555-8266
2.	Barazia	Elvira		317-40-0989	305-555-4134
3.	Dumez	Alexander	W.	384-20-9226	305-555-0372
4.	Fiorello	Jacque	R.	342-90-6321	305-555-7003
5.	Gomez-Salley	Oscar	T.	281-44-6082	305-555-5629
6.	Johnson	Monica	A.	375-15-3465	305-555-8031
7.	Kasturi	Prahlad		347-28-6385	305-555-2746
8.	London	Maria	R.	306-74-6397	305-555-6050
9.	Maas	Alexis	G.	385-64-3386	305-555-6746
10.	McGarry	Scott	J.	411-62-8120	305-555-1452
11.	Morrison	Helena	J.	236-41-1265	305-555-6473
12.	Ngan	Yi-Pheng		293-62-6113	305-555-2551
13.	Niehaus	Susan	K.	361-26-0916	305-555-5216
14.	O'Rourke	Allison	Y.	350-38-4332	305-555-6604
15.	Pace	William	D.	332-85-9163	305-555-9275
16.	Peoples	Louisa	S.	356-72-1549	305-555-4014
17.	Rezvani	Mohamed	A.	349-17-7258	305-555-9039
18.	Rodriguez	David	R.	378-62-6514	305-555-3837
19.	Savino	Durado	L.	371-77-3519	305-555-5893
20.	Schultz	Ann	G.	410-71-7295	305-555-0209
21.	Shean	Colleen		385-25-0140	305-555-2837
22.	Tomlin	Mark	E.	322-93-7708	305-555-7425
23.	Tuosto	Jennifer	K.	348-73-8900	305-555-1225
24.	Van Dyke	Kenneth	W.	246-88-9351	305-555-7135
25.	Walters	Jimmy	K.	379-93-2759	305-555-3881
26.	Wong	Matthew	D.	396-36-8265	305-555-3626
27.	Yager-Allen	Beth	A.	337-74-8423	305-555-4629
28.	Zurbrigg	Lloyd	A.	639-42-8345	305-555-2048
29.	Jarvis-Parker	Alan	M.	343-16-0891	305-555-3765
30.	Sajonas	Lea	R.	308-17-2390	305-555-8246
31.	Nealy	Jesse	J.	239-87-3885	305-555-7656

	ADDRESS	CITY	STATE	ZIP	DATE OF BIRTH
1.	1801 Windmill Lane	Winter Garden	FL	32787-2114	72/11/30
2.	1310 Foxridge Apartments	Orlando	FL	32804-3248	58/09/15
3.	2736 Calloway Street	Orlando	FL	32807-1477	45/03/26
4.	803 Westriver Avenue	Orlando	FL	32803-8454	72/06/13
5.	50 Stonegate Apartments	Eustis	FL	32726-0431	70/05/08
6.	H-1 Apartment Heights	Orlando	FL	32801-1665	72/10/19
7.	39 Bolton Drive	Orlando	FL	32802-0989	68/02/22
8.	2101 Ramble Road	Orlando	FL	32808-5012	71/07/14
9.	15 South Rosewood	Haines City	FL	33844-1122	41/11/07
10.	Route 2, Box 277	Sanford	FL	32771-1929	59/05/20
11.	1613 Palmetto Circle	Orlando	FL	32802-1255	70/04/25
12.	824 Lakeview Drive	Orlando	FL	32804-3454	62/06/21
13.	10614 Dunkirk Drive	Orlando	FL	32807-6302	53/04/18
14.	6608 Bestwicke Court	Eustis	FL	32726-1422	71/09/05
15.	1820 Park Manor Drive	Orlando	FL	32801-1274	71/07/12
16.	213 East Oak Avenue	Sanford	FL	32771-0979	47/03/16
17.	33 Mark Street	Sanford	FL	32771-2040	55/12/24
18.	911 Timberlane	Orlando	FL	32805-4220	73/02/20
19.	827 Orange Grove Road	Sanford	FL	32771-0585	64/08/27
20.	106 Stevens Road	Orlando	FL	32806-8327	70/10/18
21.	2711 Chelsea Apartments	Orlando	FL	32806-8081	60/07/22
22.	5341 Luwana Drive	Winter Garden	FL	32787-0446	71/11/19
23.	2010 Windsor Apartments	Orlando	FL	32804-3910	40/04/20
24.	363 Pine Forest Drive	Orlando	FL	32808-5144	56/09/18
25.	12821 Chestnut Street	Winter Garden	FL	32787-2206	73/03/25
26.	2540 Harrell Avenue	Eustis	FL	32726-0914	67/06/28
27.	Route 4, Box 282	Haines City	FL	33844-2174	67/08/14
28.	2910 Accokeek Road	Winter Garden	FL	32787-1484	68/01/17
29.	406 Miller Street	Eustis	FL	32726-0228	67/03/24
30.	Route 2, Box 846	Sanford	FL	32771-1207	72/11/07
31.	3224 Azalea Drive	Orlando	FL	32803-1447	73/02/11

	DATE HIRED	HOURLY WAGE	FULL/PART TIME	JOB TITLE
1.	89/04/01	5.50	Part	Salesperson
2.	83/04/15	12.30	Full	Manager
3.	85/09/12	4.80	Part	Salesperson
4.	89/11/10	4.95	Part	Line Cook
5.	88/03/20	6.25	Full	Stock Assistant
6.	89/02/18	4.60	Part	Salesperson
7.	84/07/28	7.25	Full	Shift Manager
8.	88/10/19	5.35	Full	Salesperson
9.	89/02/25	4.75	Part	Line Cook
10.	83/06/15	6.25	Full	Custodian
11.	87/05/23	5.65	Full	Line Cook
12.	82/02/18	8.90	Full	Shift Manager
13.	86/04/14	10.25	Full	Shift Manager
14.	89/02/20	4.90	Part	Salesperson
15.	88/01/01	5.40	Full	Line Cook
16.	89/03/26	4.75	Part	Salesperson
17.	86/11/24	5.30	Full	Line Cook
18.	89/03/15	4.95	Full	Salesperson
19.	84/06/15	10.45	Full	Bookkeeper
20.	89/02/10	4.95	Part	Salesperson
21.	83/08/16	6.50	Full	Stock Manager
22.	89/03/11	4.85	Part	Salesperson
23.	83/11/30	8.45	Part	Assistant Bookkeeper
24.	84/06/20	5.50	Full	Salesperson
25.	89/05/16	4.70	Part	Salesperson
26.	88/10/27	4.80	Part	Salesperson
27.	87/05/22	5.15	Full	Line Cook
28.	88/04/27	4.95	Part	Line Cook
29.	xx/xx/xx *	5.25	Full	Line Cook
30.	xx/xx/xx *	4.80	Part	Custodian
31.	xx/xx/xx *	4.60	Part	Salesperson

*These dates are to be entered by the student. They should be the dates the exercises are completed.

NOTES

NOTES

NOTES

NOTES

NOTES

E - CARRIERS

SE REGION

D - VISIBLE FILES

SC REGION

C - ACCESSORIES

NW REGION

B - FILE CABINETS

NE REGION

A - FURNITURE

NC REGION

Subject File

Geographic File

FanFile
SIDE 2

U - Z	**4000 - 4999**
P - T	**3000 - 3999**
J - O	**2000 - 2999**
E - I	**1000 - 1999**
A - D*	**0000 - 0999**
Alphabetic File	**Numeric File**

***numbers precede A**

FanFile
SIDE 1